# THE ELEMENTS
*of*
# RÉSUMÉ STYLE

SECOND  EDITION

MÉ STYLE

are in and the significant
*le* has been over the years

...........resource for job seekers at the New Haven Free Public Library in helping them to create a résumé that will really get noticed by employers. I would recommend every public library in the United States purchase a copy for their collection."

—SETH GODFREY, Business, Jobs & Non-Profit Services Librarian,
New Haven Free Public Library

"At Kinko's, we print more resumes than any other firm in the world. We see the good, the bad, and the ugly in resumes. I highly recommend Scott Bennett's book for anyone wishing to create the winning resume."

—GARY M. KUSIN, President, CEO, and Director, Kinko's Inc.

"Reading this compact volume is like getting inside the mind of a hiring manager. It should be required reading for every job applicant."

—PAT PRECIN, Managing Director, Pathways to Housing

"Absolutely outstanding. A marvelous piece of work. This book delivers what it says it will and then some. No job seeker or career changer should be without it."

—JOHN J. KENNEDY, ED.D., career development consultant

"Scott has managed the near-impossible—covering the subject from AA to ZZ. For the serious résumé writer, the sections 'Request for Salary Requirements' and 'Marketing to Yourself' alone are worth fifty times the cost of this tightly written manual."

—HERSCHELL GORDON LEWIS, direct response writer/consultant/lecturer,
and author of dozens of classic books on copy writing and advertising

"Scott Bennett presents the art and science of résumé and cover letter writing in a clear, comprehensive package that will serve as a useful tool for employment seekers. I recommend his guide to all seekers and outplacement professionals."

—BARRY NEWMARK, Director of Human Resources,
Brooklyn Bureau of Community Service

"It's rare to find professional wisdom and practical sense in the same book. Scott Bennett delivers both. As someone with years of experience in helping both students jump-start their careers and executives choose the right applicant, I know his words can make a genuine difference at whatever step of the career ladder to which you're hoping to move."

—Dr. Steve Burghardt, Professor, Organization & Planning, Hunter College School of Social Work, and Vice President, Research & Organizational Development, Leadership Transformation Group, LLC

"*The Elements of Résumé Style* provides a clear, well-marked path to construction of effective résumés and cover letters. It is a quick and easy read; the language and style make it inviting, and it is chock full of information essential to every level of job seeker. Usually these books are rough going and boring, but this one is supportive and fun. Young people in our Independent Living/Life Skills Program will be encouraged to use this wonderful resource as they enter the world of work."

—Carol M. Altomare, CSW, Director, Independent Living/Life Skills Program, Jewish Child Care Association

"The author presents the information in such a clear, concise, well-organized way. I felt like an experienced friend was helping me through tricky territory in a very candid, yet patient and kind way."

—Nina Jaffe, copyeditor, Vermont

"Bennett's writing is succinct; it's a pleasure to read. His book is a delightful mix of useful, pointed, and timely content. Great help overcoming internal demons as well as external barriers. Bravo!"

—Barbara Wood, Ph.D., VP for Pathmaker Services, Greyston Foundation

"*The Elements of Résumé Style* is a useful addition to the literature on the art of résumé writing. It contains very detailed, specific wording recommendations not found in other books on this subject. I highly recommend it."

—Robert W. Bly, copywriter/consultant/seminar leader, and author of more than 50 books on marketing, direct mail, writing, and business communication

# THE ELEMENTS

*of*

# RÉSUMÉ STYLE

## ESSENTIAL RULES FOR WRITING
## RÉSUMÉS AND COVER LETTERS THAT WORK

SECOND 2 EDITION

## Scott Bennett

**AMACOM**

AMERICAN MANAGEMENT ASSOCIATION

New York • Atlanta • Brussels • Chicago
Mexico City • San Francisco • Shanghai • Tokyo
Toronto • Washington, D.C.

This publication is designed to provide accurate and authoritative information in regard to the subject matter covered. It is sold with the understanding that the publisher is not engaged in rendering legal, accounting, or other professional service. If legal advice or other expert assistance is required, the services of a competent professional person should be sought.

ACA is a registered trademark of American Counseling Association Corp.
Adobe, Adobe Reader, Dreamweaver, and PDF are either registered trademarks or trademarks of Adobe Systems Incorporated in the United States and/or other countries.
Amazon.com and Kindle are trademarks of Amazon.com, Inc.
American Heart Association is a service mark and a registered trademark of the American Heart Association, Inc.
AMHCA is a registered trademark of American Mental Health Counseling Association.
APICS and The Association for Operations Management are registered trademarks of American Production & Inventory Control Society, Inc.
Benetton is a registered trademark of Benetton Group S.P.A. Corporation Italy.
BMW is a registered trademark of BMW AG (Bayerische Motoren Werke Aktiengesellschaft).
Dale Carnegie Training is a service mark of Dale Carnegie & Associates, Inc.
Google.com and gmail.com are service marks of Google Inc.
iVillage.com is a service mark of iVillage Inc.
Kodak is a registered trademark of Eastman Kodak Company.
Microsoft, MS-DOS, Outlook, PowerPoint, Visual Basic, Visual C++, Visual Interdev, Windows, and Windows NT are registered trademarks of Microsoft Corporation.
Myers-Briggs and Myers-Briggs Type Indicator are registered trademarks of Consulting Psychologists Press, Inc.
NAPM and Institute for Supply Management are registered trademarks of National Association of Purchasing Management.
Parents' Choice is a service mark of Parents' Choice Foundation Charitable Trust.
Ping-Pong is a registered trademark of Parker Brothers, Inc.
Red Cross is a service mark of The American National Red Cross.
Salesforce.com is a registered trademark of salesforce.com, Inc.
Self-Directed Search is a registered trademark of Psychological Assessment Resources, Inc.
Sprint is a registered trademark of Sprint Communications Company L.P.
Strong Interest Inventory is a registered trademark of Stanford University Press.
The New Yorker is a registered trademark of Advance Magazine Publishers, Inc.
Tulip is a registered trademark of Duncan Enterprises Corporation.
UPS is a registered trademark of United Parcel Service of America, Inc.
YMCA is a service mark of National Council of Young Men's Christian Associations of the United States of America.

LIBRARY OF CONGRESS CATALOGING-IN-PUBLICATION DATA
Bennett, Scott, 1962–
The elements of resume style : essential rules for writing resumes and cover letters that work / Scott Bennett. -- Second edition.
     pages cm
  Includes bibliographical references and index.
  ISBN-13: 978-0-8144-3393-5
  ISBN-10: 0-8144-3393-6
  1.  Resumes (Employment) 2.  Cover letters.  I. Title.
  HF5383.B423 2014      650.14'2--dc23      2014016984

*This book is dedicated to Jackie, Bonnie, and Wayne,*
*who share my love of words and word-free moments,*
*and to every active career seeker.*

# Contents

Preface to the Second Edition                                             xiii

## INTRODUCTION: WRITERS MAKE CHOICES                                      xv

Why Sometimes You Can Do Everything Right and Still Get No Invitation to an Interview • Pay Attention to Items Within Your Control • Less Is More • Twelve Things You Can Do Without

## 1.  COMMON CONCERNS                                                      1

Are You Sure of Where You Want to Work? • Are You Sure of What You Want to Do? • Move Beyond Your Dreamkillers • Résumé Length • Chronological or Functional Résumé? • Employment Gaps • Include Interim Jobs? • Self-Employment • Job Hopping • What About Social Media?

## 2.  PRESENTATION: THE READER SEES MORE THAN WORDS                        13

Paper • Ink • Margins • Spacing • Font • Boldface • Italics • All Caps • Underlining • Save As . . .

## 3. EVEN THE SIMPLEST ITEMS SEND MESSAGES TO THE READER    19

Your Name • Your Address • Your Phone Number • Your Fax Number • Your E-Mail Address • Your E-Mail Signature

## 4. SELL YOUR SKILLS AND EXPERIENCE—
## ALWAYS WITH THE READER IN MIND    23

Goal Section? • Goal vs. Objective • Executive Summary Section? • Give Readers a Reason to Believe • Education or Work Experience Section First? • "Work Experience" vs. "Professional Experience" • Position Descriptions/Blurbs • Sentences/Action Statements • Verbs/Action Words • Volunteer Experience Section • Education Section • Inventions, Published Works, Seminars Section • Software Skills Section • Language Skills Section • Memberships Section • References Statement? • Personal Information Section? • Artwork, Photos, Decorative Borders, and Line Art

## 5. DELIVER YOUR MESSAGE THE RIGHT WAY
## TO THE RIGHT PLACES    57

Sending Your Résumé • Job/Career Fairs and Reverse Job/Career Fairs • Responding to Blind Ads • Thinking Outside the Cubicle

## 6. COVER LETTERS    65

Cover Letters in General • Sample Response Letter • The Unsung Hero of the Job Search: The Inquiry Letter • Sample Inquiry Letter • Informational Interview Request Letter • Sample Informational Interview Request Letter

## 7. THE FINAL THREE PRE-INTERVIEW ITEMS:
## SALARY REQUIREMENTS, SALARY HISTORY, REFERENCES    73

Request for Salary Requirements • Request for Salary History • Elements of Compensation for Salary History • References

## 8. MARKETING TO YOURSELF                                    81


## 9. BONUS INTERVIEW CHAPTER, BY POPULAR DEMAND:
## SCOTT, MY RÉSUMÉ WORKED! NOW WHAT?!                       83

Physical Prep • Mental Prep • Read Up and Then Meet Up • Are You
Ready for Your Close-Up? • After the Interview


## CONCLUSION: YOU'RE THE CARPENTER                           95


## APPENDICES                                                  97

A. More Examples of Effective Position Descriptions/Blurbs     99
B. A Special Note to Homemakers                               117
C. A Special Note to Veterans                                 119
D. A Special Note to Ex-Offenders                             123
E. A Special Note to People in Recovery                       127

Index                                                         129
About the Author                                              135

# Preface to Second Edition

Paraphrasing oft-amended remarks by American author and humorist Mark Twain: Reports of the résumé's death are wildly exaggerated. More than a few present-day career writers have claimed 1) the résumé is your obituary, and 2) social media presence is who you are. Both of these claims are absurd, and here's why.

Yes, a poorly crafted résumé can resemble an obituary, and yet this was equally true way before social media, before the Internet, before personal computing, before the typewriter, and even before typesetting.

Social media—as prolific and sometimes ingenious as it is—follows venerable traditions like oral storytelling, calligraphy, handwriting, and the printing press; the typewriter, mini-computing, the word processor, PC, notebook/laptop, and tablet or smart phone; hand delivery, Pony Express, USPS ("snail mail"), fax (telecopy, facsimile), and FedEx; e-mail, e-mail attachments, word processing software (.doc, .docx), Adobe Reader (.pdf), HTML, text messages, photo formats, video formats, audio formats, QR codes, the cloud, and so much more. The foregoing comprises a teeny-tiny subset of the impressive and unending array of delivery systems past, present, and future. *Take care to not confuse content with delivery system.* Similarly, the phrase "war on terror" sounds a lot like "war on cannons" or "war on water balloons"—terror and cannons and water balloons are delivery systems, not enemies. Focus on your content at least as much as the delivery system(s), because content is what sells.

- Your error-free, clear, focused, and targeted cover letters and résumé are not your obituary.
- Your error-free, clear, focused, and targeted cover letters and résumé are not a list of what you did, that is, not a list of duties/tasks plucked from job descriptions.
- Your error-free, clear, focused, and targeted cover letters and résumé are not who you are.
- Your error-free, clear, focused, and targeted cover letters and résumé comprise your content.
- Content sells.

U.S. Supreme Court Associate Justice Elena Kagan presented the fall 2013 Albritton Lecture at University of Alabama Law School at Tuscaloosa, and in it, she touched on the subject of taking a case to the Supreme Court. Interestingly, she said an attorney's oral argument before the Court "sometimes is important," and yet she also stated, and elected to emphasize:

> I have to say, the first and the most important thing that happens in terms of one's thinking about the case, is when we receive the written brief, the document submitted in advance . . . so, for all you law students out there . . . getting your arguments down in the most persuasive form in the written materials that you give to the Court matters the most, because that's where you're really going to start thinking about a case and the arguments on each side and trying to figure out whose is stronger, so that's the most important thing.

In the same way, I encourage you to use this book to, in order of importance, (1) write your cover letters right and (2) write your résumé right, to maximize your chances to present your oral arguments in an interview.

I am grateful to the tens of thousands of active career seekers who have fruitfully worn out their copies of the first edition of this book, and I extend special thanks to those also kind enough to share their success stories. I welcome *your* success stories at bennettcenterllc@gmail.com.

# Writers Make Choices

The content of your résumé, cover letters, and other pre-interview documents is really a series of choices. This guide will provide you with an employer's perspective so you can make *informed* choices. Apply this new knowledge and you will avoid common errors, create maximum impact, and generate more responses than ever before. The choices you make as you write are crucial to generating responses. But there's more going on here.

## WHY SOMETIMES YOU CAN DO EVERYTHING RIGHT AND STILL GET NO INVITATION TO AN INTERVIEW

An error-free, clear, focused, and targeted cover letter and résumé may yield no interview for many reasons.* Here are eight:

1. As bizarre as it may sound, many organizations advertise openings already filled. Advertising such "pre-wired" jobs seems silly, but policies, contracts, or regulations often require it.

---

*However, if you've hired people yourself, you'll recognize the following inescapable math: As an employer, if you receive 200 or more résumés for an open position, maybe 10 are error-free (if you're lucky). The rest are discarded. Of the 10 without errors, only around five will be clear, focused, and targeted. These five or so folks get called for interviews. Creating an error-free, clear, focused, and targeted cover letter and résumé is within your control—and this guide will show you how to do it.

2. Some less-than-scrupulous headhunters trawl for résumés by placing an ad even when no specific position really exists, hoping to attract candidates for potential employer-clients.

3. Sudden changes (reorganizations, budget cuts, hiring freezes, or layoffs, for example) remove the need to fill an advertised opening.

4. Inefficient organizations of all sizes may take months to move from placing an ad to contacting applicants.

5. Mismatch. An employer receives enough responses from other candidates whose skills and experience appear more closely suited to a specific position.

6. Timing. A targeted inquiry reaches an organization with suitable positions but no current openings.

7. Employer idiosyncrasies. The varied preferences of decision makers mean that the most talented candidate doesn't always prevail. For example, some hiring managers reject all graduates from certain schools. Decca Record Company rejected the Beatles in 1962 and declared, "We don't like their sound, and guitar music is on the way out."

8. Lack of civility often accounts for the absence of any response (e.g., an invitation to interview or a courtesy letter, postcard, or e-mail).

Notice something in common about all these situations? The absence of an invitation to interview in such situations has absolutely nothing to do with you or your cover letter or résumé. These situations are beyond your control. Remember this, or you will mistakenly blame your cover letter or résumé or yourself for the absence of a desired response when none of these is at fault.

## PAY ATTENTION TO ITEMS WITHIN YOUR CONTROL

The trick to writing a winning cover letter and résumé is focusing carefully on the many items you *can* control.

Choose to use the tips in this guide and I believe you will increase the number of responses you receive from prospective employers. Here's why: Your compelling cover letter and résumé sent to targeted readers will convey a lot about you even before any response phone call/e-mail or in-person interview takes place. For example:

- You can organize data and thoughts.
- You can present complex information concisely.
- You pay attention to detail.
- You communicate in a clear and focused way.
- You are enthusiastic.
- You have valuable skills.

In many ways, your cover letter and résumé are the "paper interview," and only by winning the paper interview do you have a chance at an in-person one.

## LESS IS MORE

Whenever you hear someone say, "to make a long story short," do you ever get the feeling it's too late? That ship has sailed. Again, writers make choices. I am going to encourage you repeatedly to choose your words carefully. The ability to "write short" is respected by most readers, including employers. No one is hired simply to read cover letters and résumés. Everyone who reads them has plenty of other work to do, too. If you're lucky, your documents will get eight to ten seconds of the reader's eyeball time. Direct those eyeballs carefully and use your precious few seconds of attention wisely. Respect the reader's time and you'll be ahead of most candidates.

Your résumé is not intended to list every task you performed at every position. Employers know this. I repeat: *Employers know this*. It is a top-line, highlights kind of document intended to quickly give readers an honest sense of your skills, where you've been, and where you're going. It's not an autobiography. The art of the résumé is to briefly and clearly convey compelling proof of one's expertise and evoke enough enthusiasm from readers to get them to respond. If your résumé gets your phone to ring or generates an e-mail, it has done its job well.

Have you ever noticed that scantily clad models appear more alluring than nude ones? In this spirit, I encourage candidates to leave a bit of mystery; save some compelling content for the interview. Flooding recipients with too much information ("TMI") may undercut a candidate's chances of being invited to an interview. Aim to convey the information necessary and sufficient for a compelling pitch, rather than TMI.

Even though your unique story may be genuinely complex, layered, and textured, your effective résumé instead demands you get to the point. As Polonius in Shakespeare's *Hamlet* ironically observed in a long and tedious introduction, "Brevity is the soul of wit."

## TWELVE THINGS YOU CAN DO WITHOUT

1. Don't make stuff up. Embellishing or exaggerating the facts is the same as lying. When you don't do this, you can never get caught and you can feel better when your head hits the pillow at night.

2. Avoid automated résumé templates (i.e., "wizards" or other do-it-yourself and fill-in-the-blanks software). Résumés created using templates look like résumés created using templates. Your résumé is too important. These free or cheap tools are no replacement for time and thought. Remember: Employers read many résumés. Identical formats are obvious. Different candidates will quite naturally have different résumé sections: Volunteer Experience, Language Skills, Memberships, Field Placements/Internships, and many others.

3. Avoid multiple résumés. Employers want from your résumé what you would want if you were an employer: some clear sense of where you've been, what you've accomplished (i.e., solid evidence of your skills), and where you're going. One résumé provides this. Writing a different résumé for each prospective employer to "keep your options open" is a misery-making enterprise, and many employers can detect the lack of direction it represents. Instead, investigate career paths of interest to you (see Chapter 1 for ideas on how to do this) and focus on one before writing.

4. Don't load your résumé with jargon or buzzwords. Hoping their résumés will get electronically "scanned" for "keywords," some candidates insert a lot of specialized lingo. If any reader—an entry-level human resources person or any other reader who

appreciates clarity—cannot understand your words, then your résumé will not evoke the responses you seek. Electronic scanners capture plenty of relevant data from résumés that are clear and accurate rather than packed with jargon. Use no mumbo jumbo.

5. If English is not your area of expertise, don't wing it. If you don't have it already, buy and read the latest edition of *The Elements of Style* by Strunk and White (only 105 pages and around seven bucks on amazon.com) before you write. Really!

6. Don't count on your spell-check. Spell-check is not an editor: *form* vs. *from* escapes spell-check, as does *their* vs. *there* vs. *they're,* among countless other such examples. If one mistakenly types *copletion* instead of *completion,* several versions of Microsoft Word suggest replacing it with *copulation* instead of *completion.* Use a dictionary or my favorite free meta-dictionary site, *www.onelook.com.*

7. Don't skip the step of proofreading your finished product. In addition to rereading your documents from start to finish for clarity, also read them backwards to catch typos. This proven technique will help slow your reading and allow you to focus on each word.

8. Don't overlook having other qualified people review your finished product. Have your documents reviewed by at least two other people (a) who routinely hire people as part of their work and (b) whose writing skills and candor you respect. Here's the hard part: Listen to what they have to say. As writers, sometimes we have to delete cherished words and phrases to create the clearest, most focused documents. It often takes another qualified set of eyeballs to help us see this.

9. Reject free "critiques" from résumé sellers. A critique from someone whose livelihood depends on converting the critique into a résumé sale is not the kind of critique you want. Stick with reviewers who meet the criteria in item 8.

10. Don't broadcast ("blast") or post your résumé on the Web unless you are comfortable with (a) your coworkers or employers seeing it, (b) headhunters using it without your permission, and (c) format or content errors being sent hither and yon.

11. Don't send your documents to prospective employers until you have a working answering machine or voice mail on every phone number that appears on your documents. Hoping that employers will call you only when you're home is folly.

12. Don't leave a silly outgoing message on your answering machine or voice mail. If you have such a message, change it to a brief, serious, audible, and clear one (without music) before you send your documents to prospective employers. Being taken seriously is crucial to your successful search.

Mindful of the foregoing, let's now address the common concerns that often—but need not—get in the way of creating an error-free, clear, focused, and targeted résumé.

# THE ELEMENTS
*of*
# RÉSUMÉ STYLE

SECOND  EDITION

# ONE

# Common Concerns

*Everyone I know has a big "but."*
—Pee-Wee Herman, "Pee-Wee's Big Adventure"

If you break into a cold sweat, get woozy, or just feel a little uneasy when you think about writing your résumé, then rest assured: (1) You are not alone, and (2) there is hope. Here are common concerns and guidance on each.

## ARE YOU SURE OF WHERE YOU WANT TO WORK?

Many candidates for whom the answer to this question is "no" will mistakenly send responses, inquiries, and résumés scattershot, with no clear plan. Such mailings are a waste of time because employers can detect mass mailings (junk mail), broadcast faxes (junk faxes), and junk e-mail (spam) just as easily as the rest of us can.

You will receive few or no responses even with an error-free, clear, and focused résumé if you send it to the wrong places. Sending an otherwise excellent but untargeted résumé is like sending an expensive box of handmade chocolates to people with diabetes who cannot eat sweets. Targeting increases the response rate.

Identify and evaluate targets before you send your résumé. Ideas are all around you. Talk to friends and family members. Look at the categories from A to Z in the yellow (and blue) pages. Read ads—not just the Help Wanted ads—in daily and weekly newspapers. Leaf through the ads in the magazines you read. Listen to ads on your favorite radio stations. See ads on television. Use the Internet.*

Mindful of the inescapable perishability of any suggested link, the following is, at the time of this writing, a list of examples of free sites you may find helpful in exploring prospective employers.

| | |
|---|---|
| www.allexperts.com | www.news.me |
| www.amiando.com | www.newsvi.be |
| www.answers.com | news.ycombinator.com/ask |
| www.ask.com | www.99events.com |
| askville.amazon.com | www.pulse.me |
| www.digg.com/reader | www.quora.com |
| www.duckduckgo.com | reader.aol.com |
| www.eventbrite.com | www.reddit.com |
| www.feeddemon.com | www.refseek.com |
| www.feedly.com | www.rssbandit.org |
| www.feedreader.com | www.rssowl.org |
| www.flipboard.com | www.stumbleupon.com |
| www.google.com/alerts | www.theoldreader.cm |
| www.loc.gov/rr/askalib/ (Ask a Librarian @ U.S. Library of Congress) | www.twubs.com |
| | www.yahoo.com |
| www.meetup.com | www.zite.com |
| www.netvibes.com | www.zoo.com |

You can use these free resources to learn more about employers in whom you're already interested, discover new ones, and see if any are targets for an inquiry letter and résumé. Doing groundwork such as this avoids the low response rates associated with inadequate targeting.

---

*No Internet access at home or on your smart phone? Access is free at many public libraries. Are you new to the Web? Your friendly local librarian can show you in less than two minutes how easy it is to use.

Once you have identified organizations where you might want to work, forget about whether they are hiring. Learn more about them, and if you see a potential fit (i.e., if you believe your skills and enthusiasm can add value), then send them a thoughtfully prepared inquiry letter (see Chapter 6) and résumé *tout de suite*.

When examining potential targets, evaluate the cultural aspects of each prospective employer. Different organizations are at different stages of existence. Consider the excitement of helping launch a start-up vs. the relative stability of working in an established enterprise. Which setting do you prefer?

Similarly, the size of an organization has a big impact on the level of financial and human resources, as well as the level of structure in place. Would you rather work in a small company without bureaucracy but with few resources? Conversely, are you willing to tolerate some red tape to have more resources in place?

The operating principles of an organization permeate every aspect of work life in that organization. For example, the shared ownership of a clear mission, responsibility with authority, an unambiguous reporting structure, an environment of mutual respect, innovation, integrity at the top, and other factors impact heavily on job satisfaction.

The style of an organization impacts work life, too. Dress code, work schedule, and perks (from pizza and Ping-Pong to cars, jets, and expense accounts) help shape our view of the workday and reveal a lot about an organization's views on the work ethic and work/life balance.

Gain insights into these and other issues from newspaper, magazine, trade and professional journal, and online posts/articles; radio and television news reports; Internet message boards; employer home pages; and knowledgeable friends and family members. Doing so will allow you to make an informed selection of targets for your inquiry letter and résumé.

Targeted inquiry letters are so powerful that some candidates don't bother with response letters at all! These people do their reconnaissance, decide where they want to work, then methodically fax, e-mail, mail, or hand-deliver an inquiry letter and résumé to each target and call judiciously—not too often—to follow up until they're hired by one of the targets.

## ARE YOU SURE OF WHAT YOU WANT TO DO?

Web tools,* books, assessment instruments (e.g., Self-Directed Search, Strong Interest Inventory, Myers-Briggs Type Indicator), and other items exist to provide food for thought but not answers. View all results as suggestions, ideas, and examples—and nothing more. Only you can choose the best path for you.

Many people hesitate to choose and focus on a specific career path because they fear they may make a wrong decision. If you feel this way, be gentle with yourself. Gather information, make the most informed decision you can, and then support your decision by pursuing it with vigor. Focus on it like a laser beam.

Learn the requirements for entering the field. Are you willing to meet those requirements? If not, move on. If so, do everything in your power to make it happen. Make the time. Ask your loved ones for understanding and support. Get the training. Look into available grants and scholarships and student loans. Earn the certification. Pass the exams. Get the license. Find successful organizations where you can pursue your chosen path and enthusiastically target them with inquiry letters and résumé. In short, be an *active* seeker.

### What if I begin working in a new career and the quality of my work isn't very good?

When we start something new, we're not supposed to be very good at it. Babies ("toddlers") typically fall down when they first attempt to walk. We view this as normal and natural. A healthy parent praises the child's attempts and encourages more. However, when as adults we stumble just as naturally to learn new things, we can be so very unkind to ourselves. It doesn't have to be this way. When you stumble on your new path, do a

---

*For example, go to your favorite search engine (e.g., *www.google.com, www.zoo.com,* or *www.duckduckgo.com*) and search for (1) "UMO career interests game" (among results, look for link to latest edition of University of Missouri's *Career Interests Game*); (2) "US DOL career guide to industries" (among results, look for link to latest edition of *U.S. Career Guide to Industries*); and (3) "US DOL OOH" (among results, look for link to latest edition of *U.S. Occupational Outlook Handbook*). All these resources are free; use them to learn more about yourself and potential career paths.

little self-parenting. Praise your efforts. Encourage yourself. And keep trying. In this spirit, the late British author Gilbert Chesterton wrote, "A thing worth doing is worth doing poorly."

## What if one day I discover the choice I made is not the ideal path for me?

There is no such thing as an ideal path. We can only make the most informed choices we can make. Over time, as we establish ourselves in a new career, we naturally continue to weigh the positives and negatives of our choices, and if there is enough good stuff, we progress/advance along the current path. If not, we investigate new paths. If instead you are frozen in place while waiting to make the perfect choice, then consider the old saying, "Perfect can be the enemy of good enough."

Any career you choose is likely not the last career you will have between now and your demise. Lighten up. Give it your best shot, and if one day you choose to change paths, congratulate yourself on your efforts, the added experience and knowledge, and move on to your next adventure.

### MOVE BEYOND YOUR DREAMKILLERS

Many of us have people in our lives I have dubbed *dreamkillers*—people who can be depended on to repeatedly assert with vigor and zeal some supposed/purported/alleged "reasons" we cannot possibly achieve our stated goals. I encourage you to, again and again, dismiss such talk and get plenty of time and space away from the people who engage in it. The most profound end-of-life regrets are typically *not* about having tried and failed; rather, they're about having abandoned any solid, sustained attempt to achieve one's goals.

### RÉSUMÉ LENGTH

Anyone who tells you there is one hard-and-fast rule on résumé length is making it up. For obvious reasons, there is a bias among hiring managers in favor of a brief, clear, and compelling document. But this can take many forms. Many people with 20 years' work experience have a successful one-page résumé. Some people with 10 years' work experience require 1¼ pages to pitch their skills most effectively. The length of your résumé depends on the nature and number of positions you have held during your unique work life.

Do you need hard-and-fast rules to follow? Here are seven:

1. As you read each word you've written, ask yourself: Does this word contribute most efficiently to the pitch? In order to save space, you may have to replace an otherwise fine word with an equally suitable shorter one. For example, *reduce ⇨ cut, instruct ⇨ train, abolish ⇨ end, television ⇨ TV, scrutinize ⇨ examine, information ⇨ data.* You get the idea.

2. As you read each action statement you've written, ask yourself: Is this information needed to make an effective pitch?

3. If the information is needed, is there a way to convey it at least as clearly using fewer words?

4. As you look at the latest draft of your résumé, ask yourself: Am I using my eight to ten seconds of each reader's attention in the most efficient way?

5. Beware of the old adage, "Material fills the available space." If you genuinely require *part* of a second page, do not interpret the blank space on page 2 as an invitation to "spread out" and write more all over your document.

6. If you require part or all of a second page, resist the urge to include a lengthy "header" (e.g., "page 2, résumé of Scott A. Bennett continued"). Instead, a simple header or footer with only your last name and the numeral 2 (e.g., *Bennett/2*) will do, if you choose to use one at all. None is needed.

7. Do not staple pages. Stapled pages make copying more difficult for recipients and the copied pages less attractive to readers.

Some candidates mistakenly believe brevity is really only for entry-level candidates. Without exception, the most effective communicators (including—it's no coincidence—most senior-level candidates) tend to create brief résumés. The ability to communicate effectively is prized by every employer. Show employers you possess this skill by "writing short." Candidates who "write long" reveal (1) an inability to organize and convey complex information quickly and (2) disrespect for the reader's time.

A résumé is not a *curriculum vitae* (CV). A CV is generally used by academics and tends to be longer than a résumé. It includes more detailed chronologies of presentations and publications, as well as field, teaching, and research experiences and more, and can run many pages. Such length and detail are inappropriate for a résumé. By applying the tips in this guide, anyone wishing to do so can convert a CV into a clear, focused, and compelling résumé.

## CHRONOLOGICAL OR FUNCTIONAL RÉSUMÉ?

Use reverse-chronological (newest to oldest) format. Most employers prefer it because it's more direct and easier to read. Plus, employers are already in on the much-touted "secret": Functional (nonchronological) résumés are used to disguise a work history the candidate thinks needs disguising. Is this a message you want to send?

Use reverse-chronological format for any sections with chronological entries (e.g., Work Experience; Field Placements/Internships; Volunteer Experience; Education; Inventions, Published Works, Seminars).

## EMPLOYMENT GAPS

Real people often have gaps in their work histories. Don't hide gaps by extending exit dates or pushing up start dates on your résumé. People get laid off or fired. We care for children or other loved ones. We recover from illnesses, traumas, or injuries. We serve time for crimes. We go to school. We do countless other things as we move through life. All such gaps can be explained in an interview. If a hiring manager reads the résumé of an obviously skilled person with a lengthy gap, he or she will simply ask the candidate about it, not shred or burn the résumé. Be kind to yourself on this point and focus on clearly showing (through position descriptions, volunteer experience, software skills, language skills, etc.) the transferable skills you can bring to your next employer.

Re-entry after an extended gap is achievable. If you can keep up with relevant trade or professional journals or take continuing education courses during the gap, great. It's not required, though. If, for example, while working in purchasing you were able to establish vendor relationships (or, say, working in public relations you were able to establish media relationships), remember: You obviously have the skills to do it again.

A few recruiters insist that gaps are unacceptable. These few are not among the smartest in their field. Being ruled out for a position on the basis of a gap is a useful warning. You wouldn't want to work for them anyway.

## INCLUDE INTERIM JOBS?

A vice president laid off from a manufacturing firm tends bar while looking for a suitable new position. A marketing director fired from a social media company cleans houses while he searches for another marketing position. A controller whose website development firm closed takes bookkeeping assignments from a temp agency until she finds her next permanent job. Should these interim jobs be part of their résumés?

This is a decision each candidate must make.* If positions you view as interim jobs are included on your résumé, some readers will respect your work ethic and honesty. Some may exploit the information by offering a lower salary. Still others may do both.

Don't assume the worst, however. Let's say the salary range in your area for the position you seek is $60,000–$80,000. It is the rare hiring manager who will ignore the range and try to get your services for $40,000 just because he or she estimates you're earning half that much at an interim job. Yes, private-sector employers (except some non-profits, which often can't afford to pay as much, anyway) exist to maximize profits, and this includes cutting costs, but they must also compete in the marketplace to attract and *retain* qualified staff. Getting you for a few months "on the cheap" and then quickly losing you to another better-paying employer is no bargain.

If you decide to omit interim jobs from your résumé, then adhere to the spirit of truth-in-advertising: Change the Work Experience section heading to Relevant Work Experience.

---

*When completing a public-sector (government) employment application (frequently required in lieu of or in addition to a résumé), the choice is clearer: Usually, omission of any position is a violation of law.

## SELF-EMPLOYMENT

Include self-employment as you would include any other position. Do not make up inflated titles like "Chief Executive Officer" or "Chairman of the Board" for your role in a solo operation.

> 5/96–present        Self-employed, Metropolis, NY
>                              Freelance Writer and Lecturer
> [3- to 6-sentence position description/blurb here . . .]
> [Strike TAB key after present on first line and at beginning of second line.]

Many former entrepreneurs mistakenly fear that prospective employers will view them as (1) unwilling or unable to report to others and (2) failures. The first of these fears is groundless and the second is impossible. First, former entrepreneurs have been where the buck stops. They understand—perhaps more clearly than other employees—the need to quickly pitch in and get something done without endless debate. Second, while a business can be a failure, a person cannot be a failure. People don't turn into goats after a business fails. They're still successes as people.

The accomplishments of entrepreneurs (especially the lessons learned) add value to their candidacies. Such candidates are usually (by necessity) excellent multitaskers and proficient at managing limited resources. Most employers also recognize the courage, perseverance, and intensity required to launch any enterprise.

## JOB HOPPING

Why do candidates who perceive themselves as job hoppers seek résumé-writing advice? What's the one thing we know for sure about job hoppers, even before we meet them? They are already clever at getting jobs. Perhaps they are falsifying or omitting start and exit dates or using a non-chronological résumé format in an attempt to camouflage reality. Some may present real dates on a reverse-chronological format. All are convincing explainers.

Although few agree on a precise definition for "job hopper," if you view yourself as one, then prospective employers may, too. However, a couple of hops does not a bunny make. If, for example, after a year in a job you were laid off, then worked six months, then left to care for a loved one who suddenly fell ill, this is not hopping. Hopping is a continuing pattern over many years.

Even such patterns are increasingly accepted in many fields, especially if you added value at each organization and learned new skills or lessons from each experience. Interestingly, more and more candidates find it helpful to think of themselves like ballplayers or coaches, adding value and then moving from place to place within one career path or industry as the market dictates.

If over many years you hop from job to job, dissatisfied and with no obvious game plan, you can choose now to shift from disguising reality to improving it. Listen to the message your job hopping may be sending you and choose to act on it:

- Do you need to explore organizations and career paths with requirements more closely suited to your skills, interests, and values? If so, return to the sections "Are You Sure of Where You Want to Work?" and "Are You Sure of What You Want to Do?" for ideas on how to proceed.
- Do you leave jobs in anger? If so, buy and read *How to Control Your Anger Before It Controls You* by Albert Ellis and Raymond Chip Tafrate (New York: Citadel Press, 1997).

### WHAT ABOUT SOCIAL MEDIA?

Decisions on whether and how to use the exploding number and variety of social media sites—*www.linkedin.com*, *www.facebook.com*, *www. twitter.com*, among many more—are both less trivial and less dire than one may have heard.

Such decisions are less trivial than one may have heard because the exploding volume of users presents risks and opportunities for the active career seeker. A lot more eyeballs than at any other time in human history can now see one's thoughtful (i.e., useful and targeted) content. This reality unleashes untold new opportunities. For example, depending on the nature of your unique career path, social media sites may prove useful to:

- Explore/research industries
- Explore/research careers
- Explore/research employers
- Explore/research hiring managers
- Explore/research published and unpublished job leads
- Reconnect with people and grow the number of people in your network
- Establish new relationships and grow the number of people in your network
- Explore/research prospective mentors and mentees
- Use new and varied electronic venues to thoughtfully distribute your content/pitch
- Establish a personal brand by posting consistently useful content in your area of expertise

This reality also poses unprecedented risks, because the immense breadth of exposure to one's content includes the uninvited. Every post to a Facebook timeline, every tweet (i.e., message sent via *www.twitter.com*), every post to a blog (i.e., content added to an online journal, or Web log) may be seen and read by prospective employers. Given this, proceed with caution and gain mastery over privacy settings on each site.* Privacy settings vary by field on some sites. Pay attention to the default settings: Are they public or private? Some sites may redistribute user content forever, which we can agree is a long time. Respect confidentiality agreements signed with employers. Use your favorite Internet search engine (e.g., *www.google.com*, *www.zoo.com*, or *www.duckduckgo.com*) to search for yourself from time to time and monitor your professional persona.

Decisions on whether and how to use social media are also less dire than one may have heard because, at the time of this writing, many humans continue to navigate their career paths with alacrity and with no personal or professional use of social media.

---

*If, for example, you elect to reserve *www.facebook.com* and *www.twitter.com* for personal use and *www.linkedin.com* for business use, do not assume employers will abide by the same rules. If your information is available online, prospective employers desiring to see it may do so. Again, make effective use of privacy settings on each site.

Want to learn more about social media? I find *www.mashable.com* and *www.techcrunch.com* have helpful content on how to navigate social media sites.

At the time of this writing, *www.namechk.com* is a free site that allows users to simultaneously check on the availability of usernames across lots of Internet sites. If you are able to secure one username for use on many major sites, this can help you establish an easy to identify, readily recognized online brand.

Among other sites are *www.careersonar.com* and *www.branchout.com* and *friends.careercloud.com*. Each uses *www.linkedin.com* and *www.facebook.com* content to search and retrieve open positions among friends/connections.

Not unlike TV viewing for some people, use of social media and the Internet in general can rapidly turn into an overwhelmingly time-consuming enterprise if not done so in moderation. On the one hand, you may elect to allocate a maximum number of check-ins or amount of time each day on social media in order to help reduce the risk of losing track of what and who is important. On the other hand, if you are engaged in a full-time search, then focus on professional use and respect/honor your personal limits (i.e., refrain from engaging in social media 24 hours/day).

Next, we'll look beyond words and phrases to the nonobvious yet powerful presentation elements of a winning résumé.

# TWO

# Presentation: The Reader Sees More Than Words

Just as your unspoken communications (e.g., facial expressions, wardrobe) often set the tone for your spoken words and deeply affect how those words are received, there are a number of elements beyond the words in your résumé that set the tone for your written words and have great impact on the reader's level of interest and attention. Here they are.

## PAPER

So many candidates—among those who still use paper—use nonwhite paper these days that you will probably attract more attention with white paper. If you can afford it, fluorescent white 24-pound, 100 percent cotton is ideal. If not, regular bright white 24-pound bond will suffice. The choice you make here is a lot like the modest investment that home sellers make to improve the curb appeal of their home—such an investment is usually money well spent.

## INK

Print your résumé in black, the most suitable color for all pre-interview documents. If you use inks other than black, you risk not being taken seriously by employers.

Unfortunately, each time you type an e-mail address, many versions of Microsoft Word (and some other word processing software) automatically underline it and change its color from black to blue. The result inappropriately draws the reader's attention away from your name, the most important item at the top of each document. Thus, it is important to remove both the underline and the blue type from your e-mail address on each document. (You need to do this even if you have only a black-and-white printer, because when you attach your documents to an e-mail message—more on this later—the recipient will see that underline and blue print.) Here's how to do that:

1. Block (SHIFT-⇨) the e-mail address.
2. Go to Format and select Font.
3. Select Underline style: (none).
4. Select Color: Black.
5. Click OK.
6. Click ⇩ to unblock text.

If you're sending your documents by hand delivery or snail mail or fax, then the recipient typically has no way to click on an underlined blue link/hyperlink, anyway. If you think (1) a specific link is unlikely to draw the reader's attention away from your name, (2) the link is of use to the recipient, and (3) you are sending the document electronically (e.g., by e-mail), then you may elect to leave the underlined blue link as-is so your recipient can click on it to get to the link quickly and easily.

### MARGINS

Set all margins (left and right, top and bottom) to one inch. Resist the temptation to make the margins smaller than this in order to cram more text onto a page. Instead, use fewer words and choose each word carefully. Maintaining one-inch margins will help your résumé stand out from the stack.

### SPACING

After each sentence, strike the space bar only once. Some people strike it twice, and over the course of a page, this wastes a lot of valuable space.

Use tabs for uniform appearance. For example:

| 1/99–1/02 | Big Giant Company, Inc., Metropolis, NY |
|---|---|
| 12/00–1/02 | Director, Client Service |
| [3- to 6-sentence position description/blurb here . . .] | |
| 6/00–12/00 | Client Service Supervisor |
| 1/99–6/00 | Client Service Representative |

After the date and before the name of the employer, strike the TAB key, not multiple spaces. The same applies between each end date and job title. Doing so will avoid your having to play with the space bar in the hopes of eventually lining up text evenly.

If you find your text flowing onto a second page by only a few lines, here are two ways you can create extra space on the first page instead:

1. Take advantage of an optical illusion: An 8-point blank line looks a lot like the space of a regular text line. Thus, change every blank line on page 1 to 8-point type. For each blank line (each line with no text), move the cursor to the beginning of the line, SHIFT-⇨, then change the font size to 8 point. After doing this for all the blank lines, you may see your overflow text pop back onto page 1.

2. Adjust the space between characters. This is called "kerning." Here is an example:

Use kerning if and only if there is slight spillover to a second page.
[normal kerning]
Use kerning if and only if there is slight spillover to a second page.
[kerning condensed 0.2 point]

See the difference? It may seem minor, but over an entire document, the space savings are considerable. Here's how to do it:

1. Move the cursor to the beginning of your document.
2. Block (SHIFT-⇩) all text.
3. Click on Format and select Font.
4. Select Character Spacing.
5. Under Spacing, select Condense and select By: 0.2 point.
6. Click OK.
7. Click ⇩ to unblock text.

If you use kerning, (1) use it for the entire document, not just select words or phrases, and (2) condense by no more than 0.2 point, or the result will look ridiculous. Really it will.

Type the sections directly below their headings. Some candidates mistakenly waste one-third of the page by typing all the content to the right of each heading:

| Work Experience | 1/99–1/02 | Big Giant Company, Metropolis, NY |
| | 12/00–1/02 | Director, Client Service |
| | | [3- to 6-sentence position description/blurb here . . .] |
| | 6/00–12/00 | Client Service Supervisor |
| | 1/99–6/00 | Client Service Representative |

This is a waste of space. Instead, stick with the following format:

**Work Experience**

| 1/99–1/02 | Big Giant Company, Inc., Metropolis, NY |
| 12/00–1/02 | Director, Client Service |
| [3- to 6-sentence position description/blurb here . . .] | |
| 6/00–12/00 | Client Service Supervisor |
| 1/99–6/00 | Client Service Representative |

Although the first example may appear to use less space than the second example, it actually uses more once the position descriptions/blurbs are in place. The suggested format (the second example) uses space much more efficiently and still leaves plenty of room on both sides for readers to scribble comments or questions.

### FONT

Select a serif font (like Times New Roman) for your documents. Research conducted by many print advertising experts has proved such fonts are easier for readers to understand* and thus generate more responses than **sans-serif (flat)** fonts. It is tempting to play "fun with fonts," but instead stick with what is proven to work.

*Tony Antin, *Great Print Advertising: Creative Approaches, Strategies, and Tactics* (New York: John Wiley & Sons, 1993), pp. 125–126.

☹ What if the Hokey-Pokey really is what it's all about?
[Arial, a sans-serif font, proven to generate fewer responses]

☹ What if the Hokey-Pokey really is what it's all about?
[Univers, a sans-serif font, proven to generate fewer responses]

☺ What if the Hokey-Pokey really is what it's all about?
[Times New Roman, a serif font, proven to generate more responses]

### Playing "Fun with Fonts"

Some folks mistakenly think that using •bullets•, lots of different *fonts*, **bold**, *italics*, ALL CAPS, underlining, and silly ***combinations of*** *THESE* will get a reader's attention. The truth is, when we accentuate everything (or too much), we accentuate nothing. Candidates often ask, "If I don't use these tricks, what will get their attention?" Your content (i.e., your properly positioned examples of transferable skills in action) will get their attention. Content sells.

### Font Size

Use no more than two font sizes to avoid a carnival-like, disorganized appearance. Use one size for your name (16 or 18 point), and another for the rest (11 or 12 point).

Resist the temptation to use smaller font sizes in order to cram more text onto a page. Again, instead use fewer words and choose each word carefully.

### BOLDFACE

Apply **boldface** only to your name and the section headings. This will provide readers with an easy path through your information. Resist the temptation to apply **boldface** to anything else.

## ITALICS

Use *italics* only for the names of publications (e.g., *The New Yorker*) and foreign phrases, if any (e.g., *cum laude* to express "with honors").

## ALL CAPS

Don't use ALL CAPS on your résumé. They serve no constructive purpose, and many readers interpret their use as rude (i.e., the written equivalent of shouting).

## UNDERLINING

Don't use <u>underlining</u> on your résumé. Like ALL CAPS, <u>underlining</u> draws the reader's eyes away from parts of your résumé. Is there any part of your résumé from which you want the reader to look away?

## SAVE AS . . .

- Word document (i.e., .docx file format), for recipients likely to use the latest version of Word
- Word 97-2003 document (i.e., .doc file format), for recipients unlikely to use the latest version of Word
- Portable Document Format (i.e., .pdf file format), for recipients likely to have Adobe Reader software (free from *www.adobe.com*) or Kindle smart phone software (free "mobile app") or a Kindle device (from *www.amazon.com*)
- Text (i.e., .txt file format), for recipients who request it or require your résumé be sent in the body of an e-mail message. Beware: Spaces originally created using the TAB key do not always travel well from sender to recipient, so be sure to see the section in Chapter 5 on "How to Send Your Résumé in the Body of an E-Mail."

Now that you have the tools you need to help you set the tone for your words, we'll explore how even items as simple as contact information send messages to the reader.

# THREE

# Even the Simplest Items
# Send Messages to the Reader

Like in many realms of life, little things mean a lot on your résumé, too.

## YOUR NAME

If your name ends in "Jr." or "II" or "III" or "IV" and so on, you may elect to omit such designation from your résumé. When these designations are used, readers may perceive you as defining yourself largely in terms of your relationship to someone else, and this may be viewed less favorably in the United States than in other countries. If you share a phone number with another person whose identity is frequently confused with yours, you are in a tough spot and you may have to include the designation. Avoid it if you can.

Do not attempt to disguise your gender or ethnicity (or the appearance of a particular ethnicity) by using initials instead of names. However, if you are really called by your initials, then place them in quotes and in parentheses:

**Julio ("J.T.") Bennett**

Omit academic degrees (e.g., AA, AS, BA, BFA, BS, DDS, DO, DVM, EdD, JD, MA, MBA, MD, MFA, MLS, MS, MSW, PhD) from your name on the résumé. Your identity and your degrees are two different things. There's a home for this information in the Education section. Avoid duplication.

## YOUR ADDRESS

If you live in an apartment, include your apartment number on your résumé. Many candidates mistakenly think a house address appears more prestigious than an apartment address, so they omit this information. However, mail is easily delayed or lost when the apartment number is missing, so include it in your address.

If you can, avoid using a post office box for an address. It implies instability and impermanence to the reader.

Do not spell out the name of your state. Use the generally accepted two-letter capitalized postal abbreviation. You have at most 10 seconds of your reader's eyeball time. Don't waste a second on trivia.

If you do not know it already, get your nine-digit Zip code from an article of incoming mail, from *www.usps.com*, or from your local post office. Using it is a sign that you pay attention to detail, a valued skill.

## YOUR PHONE NUMBER

Include your home and/or personal cell phone number. Not your work phone. Not a cell phone paid for by your employer. Callers can generally infer from the outgoing voice mail message on an employer-paid phone that it is an employer-paid phone. You do not want to be perceived as someone who uses—and will use—an employer's time and resources to find another job.

Do not include pager numbers of any kind, business or personal. Make responding easy for the reader.

Use a few Internet search engines (e.g., *www.google.com*, *www.zoo. com*, or *www.duckduckgo.com*) to learn if, and in what context, your phone number appears on the Web. If you're unable to have the number removed from irrelevant or undesirable content and you want to prevent prospective employers from seeing it there, then procure a new number for use on your cover letters, résumé, and all job search correspondence. For example, a local number in a United States area code with unlimited calling to United States and Canada costs, at the time of this writing, approximately US$60 per year from Skype (*www.skype.com*), including the ability to access voice mail messages from a variety of devices.

### YOUR FAX NUMBER

If you have a home fax number, list it. Do not use an employer's fax number.

### YOUR E-MAIL ADDRESS

An e-mail address implies comfort with computers. If you have a personal e-mail address you check daily, then list it. If you don't check daily, do not. If your personal e-mail address is silly, create a new and more appropriate one. (At the time of this writing, free e-mail is available at *www.gmail.com*, *www.yahoo.com*, *www.outlook.com*, and other sites.) In order to be contacted, you must first be taken seriously. Use this new e-mail address for sending résumés to prospective employers and check it for new mail daily. Do not send from one address and ask recipients to respond to—by having to type or cut and paste—another address. Again, make responding easy for the reader.

Again, use a few Internet search engines (e.g., *www.google.com*, *www.zoo.com*, or *www.duckduckgo.com*)  to learn if, and in what context, your e-mail address appears on the Web. If you are unable to have the address removed from irrelevant or undesirable content and you want to prevent prospective employers from seeing it there, then obtain a new e-mail address for use on your cover letters, résumé, and all job search correspondence.

### YOUR E-MAIL SIGNATURE

Look for Settings or Options in your e-mail application and then look for "e-mail signature" to create the content you want to appear at the end of every message you send. You're limited only by your creativity/ingenuity/imagination. The e-mail signature is valuable real estate most candidates ignore. You may elect to include in your e-mail signature a link to your content/pitch for the people in your network . . . and others, too. Once your e-mail signature is set up, remember this: Unless you delete it, your e-mail signature is automatically included in every e-mail message you send. I repeat: Unless you delete it, your e-mail signature is automatically included in *every* e-mail message you send. Exceptions: A few e-mail applications provide options related to inclusion of e-mail signature(s). Microsoft Outlook, for example, has different options depending upon whether a user is creating a new message, replying, or forwarding. Thus, Outlook users can set those options to different signatures—or say, none on reply/forward—as desired.

———

The more attention you give to such details, the less work you ask your reader to do. When reading résumés, hiring managers sometimes feel like the Rodney Dangerfields of the work world: They get no respect. Be the exception; sweat the details and respect your reader.

# FOUR

# Sell Your Skills and Experience— Always with the Reader in Mind

We all long to be understood. Yet we know in life that a message received is often very different from the message sent. As you craft every section of your résumé, think about the receiver of your sales message so that your skills and experience—your unique story—can be easily and rapidly understood.

## GOAL SECTION?

The only people who need a Goal section on their résumés are those who are changing careers. If you are not changing careers, do not include a Goal section. If you are changing careers, then give the goal a lot of thought because this (brief!) item must clearly state your intent to transition from your past work experience to your desired work experience.

A goal statement need not exceed two sentences. Keep in mind: Transferable skills are what matter, and those will be clear from your position descriptions/blurbs and other sections. Keep your goal statement brief. For example, "Transition to and establish career in X" may serve as a suitable goal statement.

Avoid a common error: Do not use "To" as the first word in a goal. Instead, begin every sentence on your résumé, including your goal (if you need one), with a verb/action word.

## GOAL VS. OBJECTIVE

Both "goal" and "objective" convey the same information, but the latter takes longer to read. *Goal* conveys the needed information and respects the reader's time.

## EXECUTIVE SUMMARY SECTION?

A summary at the top of a résumé is often interpreted to mean, "My résumé is kind of long and tedious. Here is the good stuff you really need to know about me, so you need not actually read the whole document." Is this an admission you want to make? Properly written, your résumé *is* a summary. If it needs summarizing, then it needs work.

## GIVE READERS A REASON TO BELIEVE

Despite our best intentions, sometimes our wording is too vague to be taken seriously—and in the absence of clear evidence, vague claims are usually interpreted as empty claims.

Most of the résumés employers receive are loaded with vague claims. Avoid such claims and your résumé will stand out from the stack. See examples in Figure 4-1.

### FIGURE 4-1. VAGUE CLAIMS TO AVOID.

| | | |
|---|---|---|
| Able | Astute | Clean* |
| Active | Attentive | Clearheaded |
| Adaptable | Attractive | Clever |
| Adept | Brilliant | Committed* |
| Aggressive | Bubbly | Compassionate |
| Alert* | Businesslike | Competent |
| Amazing | Calm* | Competitive |
| Ambitious | Capable | Confident |
| Amiable | Careful | Conscientious |
| Analytical | Cautious | Conservative |
| Appealing | Charitable | Consistent |
| Articulate* | Charming | Coolheaded |
| Assertive | Cheerful | Cooperative |

| Courageous | Generous | Original |
| Courteous | Goal-oriented | Outgoing |
| Creative | Gregarious | Patient* |
| Curious | Hands-on | People-oriented |
| Customer-oriented | Hardworking | People-person |
| Daring | Healthy | Perceptive |
| Decisive | Helpful | Persevering |
| Dedicated* | High-energy | Persistent |
| Dependable | Honest | Personable |
| Detail-minded | Humble | Persuasive |
| Detail-oriented | Humorous | Pleasant |
| Determined* | Imaginative | Poised |
| Diligent | Independent | Positive |
| Diplomatic | Industrious | Practical |
| Disciplined* | Innovative | Proactive |
| Discreet | Instrumental | Productive |
| Eager | Introspective | Professional |
| Easygoing | Introvert | Proficient |
| Effective | Judicious | Receptive |
| Effervescent | Kind | Reliable |
| Efficient | Knowledgeable | Resilient |
| Eloquent | Levelheaded | Resourceful |
| Energetic | Logical | Responsible |
| Enterprising | Loving | Results-driven |
| Enthusiastic | Loyal | Results-oriented |
| Ethical | Mature | Sassy |
| Excellent | Methodical | Savvy |
| Experienced* | Meticulous | Seasoned* |
| Extrovert | Modest | Self-confident |
| Fabulous | Motivated* | Self-managing |
| Fair | Multitasking | Self-motivated |
| Fantastic | Neat | Self-reliant |
| Firm* | Objective | Self-starter |
| Flexible | Obliging | Sense of humor |
| Forceful | Open-minded | Sensitive |
| Frank | Optimisitic | Sharp |
| Friendly | Organized* | Sincere |

(continues)

**FIGURE 4-1. VAGUE CLAIMS TO AVOID.** (continued)

| | | |
|---|---|---|
| Sophisticated | Swell | Vivacious |
| Spectacular | Tactful | Well-groomed |
| Strong | Takes initiative | Well-organized |
| Suave | Talented | Wonderful |
| Successful | Team player | Zestful |
| Supportive | Tenacious | Zippy |

*Do not use as an adjective/descriptive word.

Why write such vague and unconvincing claims when specific action statements provide quick and powerful evidence of valuable skills? For example, compare "Excellent written communications skills" and "Wrote jargon-free *User Guide* for 11,000 users." Do you see the crucial difference? The former is hollow self-puffery; the latter, credible evidence of a valuable skill. See Figure 4-2 for more examples.

As you write:

* Avoid vague claims.
* Use brief, specific examples to demonstrate—rather than merely claim—skills.

**FIGURE 4-2. HOLLOW SELF-PUFFERY VS. EVIDENCE OF USEFUL SKILLS.**

| Vague Claims, Viewed by Readers as Hollow Self-Puffery | Specific Action Statements, Viewed by Readers as Evidence of Valuable Skills |
|---|---|
| Experience working in fast-paced environment. | Registered 120+ third-shift emergency room patients/night. |
| Excellent verbal skills. | Trained 30 new hires on customer service protocols. |
| Confident and poised. | Developed and presented cost-reduction plan to board of directors. |

| Team player with cross-functional awareness. | Collaborated with clients, A/R, and Sales to increase speed of receivables and prevent interruption of service to clients. |
| --- | --- |
| Rare combination of superior interpersonal skills and in-depth technical skills understanding. | Translated complex changes into jargon-free written updates for nontechnical users in 4 countries. |
| Provided a broad-based flow of data. | Interpreted survey results to create 16 unique monthly reports for Sales, Marketing, and Finance. |
| Dedicated hands-on management style. | Cut annual employee turnover rate 85% (from 40%/year to 6%/year) in 36 months. |
| Demonstrated success in analyzing client needs. | Created and implemented comprehensive needs assessment mechanism to help forecast demand for services and staffing. |
| Make well-thought-out decisions. | Created RFPs with clear requirements, evaluated complex results, and selected new suppliers. |

## EDUCATION OR WORK EXPERIENCE SECTION FIRST?

If you are attending or recently completed vocational school, college, or graduate school and have little relevant work experience, place your Education section first. If you have a lot of relevant work experience (even if you recently returned to school), place the Work Experience section first.

## "WORK EXPERIENCE" VS. "PROFESSIONAL EXPERIENCE"

Both terms convey the same information, but the latter takes longer to read. "Work Experience" says what is needed and respects the reader's time.

"Experience" alone (without "Work" or "Professional") is ideal, but only on résumés with no Volunteer Experience section.

No colon is required after this heading or any other section heading on your résumé.

## POSITION DESCRIPTIONS/BLURBS

When the starting month and year and ending month and year are omitted from an entry, readers may infer (1) an attempt to disguise gaps (whether or not the candidate is doing so), (2) the candidate has a poor memory, or (3) the candidate is too lazy to retrieve the information. None of these is a desirable message to send. Include the starting month and year and ending month and year for each entry.

In the United States, there is no zero used to express any of the months, except in "10" to represent October. For example, "January 2003 through July 2005" is written "1/03–7/05," not "01/03–07/05," and not "January 2003 through July 2005"—also a waste of the reader's time.

Omit the street addresses and Zip codes of employers. The city and state will do. Plus, resist the temptation to change the name of any employer or other organization from text to a link. A link invites and encourages readers to instantly navigate away from your document with just one click.

> 1/99–1/02          Big Giant Company, Inc., Metropolis, NY
> [Strike TAB key after end date.]

Think outside the cubicle; replace parochial "internal speak" position titles with titles outsiders can easily understand. If, for example, your internal title is CSR4, then write an accurate and understandable equivalent instead (e.g., Senior Customer Service Representative). Make understanding easy for the reader.

Exclude bullets. Long ago, bullets were intended to precede a single word. Over time people stretched their use to phrases, then whole thoughts, then paragraphs with connecting thoughts. Nowadays, bullets waste space on a résumé. Neither a bullet nor any other symbol will propel a reader's eyes and interest on a résumé as quickly as a thoughtful and succinct paragraph. Use from three to six sentences/action statements in a paragraph to construct a position description/blurb for each position.

On an 8½ × 11-inch résumé page with one-inch margins, a position description/blurb as long as the preceding paragraph would (1) save space and (2) require readers to move their eyes from left to right five times. This is faster and easier—37.5 percent fewer eye movements—than reading the same words with bullets. Look at the points made in the previous paragraph, now presented instead in a bulleted list:

- Exclude bullets.
- Long ago, bullets were intended to precede a single word. Over time people stretched their use to phrases, then whole thoughts, then paragraphs with connecting thoughts.
- Nowadays, bullets waste space on a résumé.
- Neither a bullet nor any other symbol will propel a reader's eyes and interest on a résumé as quickly as a thoughtful and succinct paragraph.
- Use from three to six sentences/action statements in a paragraph to construct a position description/blurb for each position.

On an 8½ × 11-inch résumé page with one-inch margins, a position description as long as the preceding bulleted list—the format used by most candidates—would (1) waste space and (2) require readers to move their eyes from left to right eight times. This is slower and more difficult—60 percent more eye movements—than reading the same words in a paragraph. Avoid both problems and stand out from most candidates: Make understanding easy for the reader and make the most effective use of your eight to 10 seconds of the reader's attention by using thoughtful and succinct paragraphs for position descriptions.

Some positions, especially the more junior or less recent ones with obvious titles, require no descriptive blurb at all. Every reader knows what a cashier or a waiter does, for example. There's no need to list each task.

If you held the same position in two or more organizations, just one descriptive blurb may be required. There are exceptions, however; each case is unique. For example, a candidate who has worked as an emergency room nurse at three urban public hospitals may require only one blurb, while a candidate who has worked as an emergency room nurse at one tribal hospital, one suburban private hospital, and one urban public hospital may require three blurbs.

When writing about positions assigned through a temporary agency, candidates often mistakenly list their work sites as their employers. Doing this is not only inaccurate but also may later be seen as an attempt to intentionally misrepresent the facts. Your employer is the organization that funds your payroll checks; this is usually the agency. Work sites are appropriately named in the blurb, especially if they are particularly prestigious.

Exclude the word *I* from your résumé. Start every sentence with a verb/action word. Remember to include cooperative verbs, too. For example, "Co-created X," "Participated in development of X," "Collaborated with A and B on X," and like phrases tell employers you play well with others.

Look beyond the usual for the strongest and most accurate action words. Some examples from the list shown in Figure 5 (presented later) are *adapt, analyze, cultivate, defuse, enhance, familiarize, foster, harness, initiate, interpret, navigate, nurture, persuade, streamline, synthesize,* and *target.* Use present-tense verbs (e.g., *write*) as appropriate for your current position and past-tense verbs (e.g., *wrote*) for all previous positions.

Save space:

- Although in other documents the numbers 1 through 9 are often expressed in words, in résumé blurbs these numbers may be expressed using numerals (e.g., 1, 2, 3…) instead.
- The numbers 10 and above may be expressed using numerals as well (e.g., 40, 800, and 12,000).
- When referring to monetary values, use *K* to express "thousands" (e.g., $20K instead of $20,000, $20 thousand, 20 thousand dollars, or twenty thousand dollars).
- When referring to monetary values, use *M* to express "millions" (e.g., $20M instead of $20,000,000, $20 million, 20 million dollars, or twenty million dollars).
- The phrase "more than" may be expressed by adding a plus (+) to a number (e.g., "Wrote *XYZ Quarterly* for 500+ staff" instead of "Wrote *XYZ Quarterly* for more than 500 staff").
- The word *approximately* may be expressed using the symbol (~) instead (e.g., "Wrote ~$300K in successful grant proposals" instead of "Wrote approximately $300K in successful grant proposals").
- The word *percent* may be expressed using the symbol (%) instead (e.g., "Achieved record-setting 117% of annual sales quota").

- The word *per* may be replaced with the forward slash (/) (e.g., "Achieved fivefold sales increase—from $120K to $720K/year").
- If necessary, the word *and* may be expressed using the forward slash (/) as well (e.g., "Analyzed 50 businesses owned/operated by consumers with mental illnesses").

### More Words and Phrases to Avoid

Why write "utilize" when "use" is simpler and more direct? Why write "Was responsible for office management" when "Managed office" is more active and more direct?

If *any* of the words or phrases in Figure 4-3 are on your résumé, then cut them out and rewrite your sentences so they are simpler and more direct.

**FIGURE 4-3. MORE WORDS AND PHRASES TO AVOID.**

| | | |
|---|---|---|
| A | Basically | Commence |
| Accompany (use *escort*) | Because | Competency |
| Accumulate | Benchmark | Concerning (use *on* or |
| Actually | Best of breed | *about*) |
| Add value | Best practice | Conciliate (use *recon-* |
| Am | Big picture | *cile*) |
| Ameliorate (use | Blaze | Consequently |
| *improve*) | Bleeding edge | Constitute (use *form*) |
| An | Brainstorm | Core |
| Appease | Broad-based | Countless |
| Architect (as a verb) | Business logic | Cross-functional |
| Are | Buy in | Currently (use *now*) |
| Ascertain (use *discover* | Carry out | Cutting edge |
| or *learn* or *determine*) | Catalyst | Cycle |
| Assume | Cease (use *stop* or *end*) | Deal (as a verb) |
| At the present time (use | Challenge | Decrease (use *cut*) |
| *now*) | Charge | Deliverable |
| Avoid (use *avert*) | Client-focused | Dialogue (as a verb) |
| B to B | Clone (unless you are in | Disincent (not a word) |
| Ballpark (as a verb) | science) | Dissect (unless you are in |
| Bandwidth | Command | science, use *examine*) |

(continues)

**FIGURE 4-3. MORE WORDS AND PHRASES TO AVOID.** (continued)

Disseminate (use *publish* or *send out*)

Downsize

Dream

Drill down

Due to the fact that

Duties

Economize

Ecosystem

Effectuate

Elucidate (use *clarify* or *explain* or *unravel*)

Empower

Empowering

Empowerment

Endeavor

End result

Excellence

Fast-track

Figure (as a verb, use *calculate*)

Final outcome

Fine-tune

Fire (as a verb; use *dismiss* or *replace*)

Float (as a verb)

Following (use *after*)

For the purpose of (use *for*)

Fortify (use *strengthen*)

Front line

Function (as a verb; use *serve*)

Functionality

Game plan

Gap analysis

Globalization

Going forward

Go public

Group (as a verb)

Guarantee (as a verb)

Hardball

Harmonize (unless you are in music)

Harvest (unless you are in farming/science)

Head (use *lead*)

Her

High level

His

I

In reference to

In the event that (use *if*)

In the loop

Incent (not a word)

Indeed

In-depth study

Indicate

Interact

Interface (as a verb)

Interpersonal

Interrelated

Is

Just

Keep (use *retain*)

Keynote (as a verb)

Knowledge base

Leadership

Leading edge

Leverage

Little

Lower (use *cut* or *reduce*)

Manipulate

Many

Me

Memorize

Mindset

Mine

Mission

Mitigate (use *ease*)

Moreover

Move the ball

Moving forward

My

Myriad

Necessitate

Numerous

Objective (use *goal*)

Offline

Off-site

Orientate (use *orient*)

Our

Out-of-pocket

Out of the box

Out of the loop

Outline (as a verb; use *summarize*)

Outside the box

Oversee (use *supervise* or *manage*)

Paradigm

Parameter

Paramount

Particularly

Past experience

Perfect (as a verb or an adjective)

Peruse (use *review*)

Point in time

Possess (use *own*)

Possibility

Preplan (unless you are in the fire service; use *plan*)

Preventative (use *preventive*)

Proactively

Problem-solve

Prototype (as a verb)

Quality-driven

Quite

Really

Rectify (use *correct* or *amend*)

Regarding (use *on* or *about*)

Reinforce

Remainder (unless you are in publishing)

Remediate

Remember

Remunerate (use *compensate* or *pay*)

Repeat

Responsibilities

Responsible for

Re-vision

Revisit

Right-size

Roll up sleeves

Schema

School (as a verb; use *educate* or *train*)

Scope (as a verb)

Set up

Simulate

Smart-size

So

Solutions

Spearhead (use *initiate* or *lead*)

Spell out

State-of-the-art

Strategize (use *plan*)

Subsequently

Substantiate (use *prove* or *verify*)

Such

Suggest (use *propose*)

Target audience

Team (as a verb)

Team building

That

There

This

Thought leader

Time frame

Tolerate

Totally

Total quality

Touch base

Transmogrify (use *transform*)

Transpire

Undertake

Underwrite (use *sponsor*)

Until such time as (use *until*)

Utilize (use *use*)

Value-added

Verbalize

Verbally

Very

Viable

Viable alternative

Virtual

Vision (as a verb)

Visioning

Visualize

Was

Well

Were

Which

Win-win

World-class

www

The blurb is not intended to list everything you did in each position. Employers know this. I repeat: *Employers know this.* Be terse and pithy. Get to the point. Stick to the highlights. A descriptive blurb is not a job description. In fact, if you are using a copy of a job description to help you write your résumé, throw it away. Instead, as you write a blurb for each position, think beyond your specific tasks and your department:

- In what ways does your work impact other departments?
- In what ways does your work contribute to the overall success of the organization?
- Have you identified problems and solved them? If so, give brief examples.
- Have you identified opportunities and acted on them? If so, give brief examples.
- Have you worked collaboratively? If so, what did doing so accomplish?
- Pretend you're the reader. As an employer, what would you want to know?
- What brief example shows/proves my skills and experience can add value for the reader?
- What brief example shows/proves my skills and experience can make the reader look good?
- What brief example shows/proves I possess traits valuable to the reader?
- What brief example shows/proves my interpersonal skills?
- What brief example shows/proves my analytical skills?
- What is in it for the reader—not for me—if s/he hires me?

What's your "elevator speech"? If you ran into a prospective employer in an elevator, how would you describe the highlights of what you do in three or four concise sentences, before the elevator arrives at the employer's floor? Think about it. Once you've figured this out, drop the word *I* from each sentence and, *voilà*, you have the blurb for your present position.

### Sample Position Descriptions/Blurbs

1/00–present          writeresumesright.com, Metropolis, NY
                              General Manager (part-time)
Provide free career resources. Write articles on résumé writing and interview skills. Select for inclusion useful information (sites, books, and software) on self-assessment, career exploration, salary negotiation, self-employment, education, and jobs (for profit, public, and non-profit).

Do not justify (even lines on the right-hand side) the blurbs. An aligned left edge with a ragged right edge is much easier to read.

9/00–3/01          XYZ Foundation, Metropolis, NY
                   Career Developer
Provided comprehensive career counseling to staff at all levels and to clients, including formerly homeless, ex-offenders, persons living with HIV/AIDS/mental illnesses, recovering from substance abuse, and moving from welfare to work. Compiled and distributed job data and resources related to literacy, learning disabilities, credit counseling, driver training, job preparedness, and vocational training. Launched JobLand career counseling office.

11/97–5/99         ABC College School of Business, Metropolis, NY
                   Career Services Counselor
Launched Career Services Office. Facilitated workshops for and counseled 2,000+ students and alumni on résumés, cover letters, pre-interview research, interviews, and post-interview follow-up skills. Developed mailings, broadcast faxes, job bank, job search training materials, and annual résumé book.

4/92–4/96          Public Service Computer Software, Metropolis, MA
8/94–4/96          President and Chief Operating Officer
Published country's best-selling administrative and educational software for firefighters. Published 3 educational software titles for kids age 11 and older: *UpFront Sex, Drugs, and Rock & Roll* (awarded Parents' Choice Honors), *UpFront Geography: You Can't Get There from Here*, and *UpFront History: What'd That Dead Guy Do?*
6/93–8/94          Sales and Marketing VP
Expanded number of users from 2,000 to 11,000+. Collaborated with technical team to meet complex and frequently changing local, state, and federal client specifications.
4/92–6/93          Sales Manager

Notice that there is no blurb for Sales Manager. A blurb is not always required for every position. In this case, the blurb for Sales and Marketing VP conveys an overview of sales achievement.

Notice also that present-tense verbs/action words are used for a current position and past-tense verbs/action words for past positions.

On an 8½ × 11-inch résumé page with one-inch margins, none of the sample blurbs uses more than six lines of text—the most that's needed to convey the highlights of nearly any position. See Appendix A for more examples of effective position descriptions/blurbs.

## SENTENCES/ACTION STATEMENTS

The action statements in each blurb represent examples of the skills you can bring to bear wherever you work. The power of these examples is at the heart of a winning résumé. Make each action statement clear, pack it with compelling evidence of your relevant skills, and keep it brief. See Figure 4-4.

### FIGURE 4-4. SENTENCES/ACTION STATEMENTS.

- Achieved $X in weekly sales.
- Achieved sixfold sales increase—from $120K to $840K/year.
- Co-chaired Continuous Quality Improvement Team.
- Co-developed system to streamline O and P.
- Collaborated with materials vendors to cut lead times in half. (The phrase "in half" is more quickly read than "by 50%." Similarly, for example, "tripled" is a quicker and more powerful read than "increased by 200%.")
- Completed M ahead of deadline and under budget.
- Conducted disaster-recovery training for X staff.
- Cut average accounts receivable from 62 to 38 days.
- Cut monthly expenses X% to $X.
- Defined and implemented procedures to serve E, F, and G.
- Defused tensions and promoted collaboration among sales and market research staffs, yielding faster, more relevant research.
- Designed recruitment literature and managed its production and distribution.
- Doubled monthly sales to $X.
- Evaluated and recommended J.
- Evaluated and selected K.
- Extracted relevant data from H to create timely I.

- Fostered collaboration among W, X, and Y to increase Z.
- Identified prospects. Closed $X in new business in first year.
- Increased annual sales X% to $X.
- Initiated and developed procedures to accelerate communication among L, M, and N.
- Initiated and implemented outsourcing of payroll, reducing administrative costs by $X/year.
- Introduced and enforced protocols for B, C, and D.
- Managed $X annual budget.
- Managed high volume of I.
- Managed introduction, pricing, promotion, and branding of Q.
- Managed migration of U system from mainframe to client/server environment.
- Managed relationships with D, E, and F.
- Managed X staff.
- Met complex local, state, and federal requirements.
- Met time-sensitive requirements of G and H.
- Nurtured small business clients, moving several from under $X to more than $Y/year.
- Participated in development of A.
- Performed outreach to J and K.
- Persuaded colleagues at corporate headquarters to replace retiring domestic fleet vehicles with more fuel-efficient imports, saving $X/year.
- Persuaded R and S to collaborate on new T strategy.
- Produced content for, maintained, and marketed X websites.
- Provided seamless transition to successor.
- Quadrupled annual sales to $X.
- Recruited, extensively trained, and remotely supervised X.
- Reduced expenses $X/year.
- Scrutinized expense reports to identify errors. Trained staff on proper expense reporting to prevent recurrences.
- Selected sites and managed complex logistics for X trade shows.
- Served as liaison among V, W, and Y to develop Z.
- Streamlined in-house recruiting function, reducing average vacancy time frame by 14 days.

(continues)

**FIGURE 4-4. SENTENCES/ACTION STATEMENTS.** (continued)

- Successfully integrated 2 culturally disparate sales forces and streamlined processes, resulting in X% margin increases and smaller staff able to serve X% more customers.
- Synthesized survey results from multiple sources to develop clear system requirements.
- Thrived amid X mergers/acquisitions. (Instead of explaining complex ownership and organizational changes, this brief sentence lets readers easily infer your flexibility and relationship skills.)
- Trained X staff on service protocols and quality measurement.
- Tripled seasonal sales to $X.
- While continuing to serve as X, also managed A, B, and C.
- Wrote detailed specs and jargon-free *User Guide* for L.

## VERBS/ACTION WORDS

Begin every action statement of every blurb with an action word. See Figure 4-5. Shop here for the most accurate and powerful action words to briefly describe your achievements. Choose your action words with care.

**FIGURE 4-5. VERBS/ACTION WORDS.**

| | | | |
|---|---|---|---|
| Abolish | Address | Air | Answer |
| Absorb | Adhere | Alert | Anticipate |
| Accelerate | Adjudicate | Align | Appeal |
| Accept | Adjust | Allay | Appear |
| Access | Administer | Allocate | Apply |
| Accomplish | Admit | Allow | Appoint |
| Accredit | Adopt | Ally | Appraise |
| Accrue | Advance | Alter | Apprehend |
| Achieve | Advertise | Amass | Apprise |
| Acquaint | Advise | Amaze | Approach |
| Acquire | Advocate | Amend | Appropriate |
| Act | Affirm | Amplify | Approve |
| Activate | Affix | Analyze | Arbitrate |
| Adapt | Aid | Anchor | Arouse |
| Add | Aim | Announce | Arrange |

| | | | |
|---|---|---|---|
| Arrest | Borrow | Centralize | Commission |
| Articulate | Brace | Certify | Commit |
| Ascend | Braid | Chair | Communicate |
| Ask | Breed | Champion | Compare |
| Assemble | Bridge | Change | Compensate |
| Assert | Brief | Channel | Compete |
| Assess | Bring | Chart | Compile |
| Assign | Broadcast | Charter | Complement |
| Assist | Broaden | Check | Complete |
| Assure | Budget | Choose | Comply |
| Attain | Build | Choreograph | Compose |
| Attend | Buoy | Chronicle | Compost |
| Attract | Buy | Circulate | Compound |
| Audit | Calculate | Circumvent | Compress |
| Augment | Calibrate | Cite | Compute |
| Authenticate | Call | Claim | Computerize |
| Author | Calm | Clarify | Conceive |
| Authorize | Campaign | Classify | Concentrate |
| Automate | Cancel | Clean | Conceptualize |
| Avert | Canvass | Clear | Conclude |
| Award | Capitalize | Climb | Condense |
| Bake | Capture | Clip | Conduct |
| Balance | Care | Close | Confer |
| Barter | Carry | Clothe | Configure |
| Bathe | Carve | Coach | Confine |
| Beat | Cash | Co-author | Confirm |
| Begin | Cast | Cobble | Conform |
| Best | Catalog | Co-chair | Confront |
| Bid | Catapult | Co-create | Connect |
| Bill | Catch | Code | Conserve |
| Bind | Categorize | Collaborate | Consider |
| Blanket | Cater | Collate | Console |
| Blend | Cause | Collect | Consolidate |
| Block | Caution | Combine | Construct |
| Bolster | Cede | Comfort | Consult |
| Book | Celebrate | Commemorate | Consummate |
| Boost | Cement | Commend | Contact |

(continues)

**FIGURE 4-5. VERBS/ACTION WORDS.** (continued)

| | | | |
|---|---|---|---|
| Contain | Debit | Detain | Divide |
| Contest | Debug | Detect | Document |
| Continue | Decentralize | Deter | Dominate |
| Contract | Decide | Determine | Donate |
| Contrast | Decipher | Develop | Double |
| Contribute | Declare | Devise | Draft |
| Control | Decline | Devote | Dramatize |
| Convene | Decode | Diagnose | Draw |
| Convert | Decorate | Diagram | Dress |
| Convey | Dedicate | Differentiate | Drill |
| Convince | Deduce | Direct | Drive |
| Cook | Deepen | Disband | Dry |
| Cooperate | De-escalate | Disburse [funds] | Duplicate |
| Coordinate | Defend | Discern | Earn |
| Copy | Defer | Discharge | Ease |
| Copyedit | Define | Discipline | Eclipse |
| Correct | Deflect | Disclose | Edge |
| Correlate | Defuse | Discontinue | Edit |
| Correspond | Delegate | Discover | Educate |
| Counsel | Delight | Discuss | Effect |
| Count | Delineate | Dismantle | Elaborate |
| Cover | Deliver | Dismiss | Elect |
| Craft | Demonstrate | Dispatch | Electrify |
| Create | Demystify | Dispense | Elevate |
| Credit | Depict | Disperse [crowds] | Elicit |
| Criticize | Deploy | Display | Eliminate |
| Critique | Depose | Dispose | Elude |
| Cull | Deposit | Disprove | Embed |
| Cultivate | Depreciate | Dispute | Embrace |
| Curb | Deprive | Dissolve | Emerge |
| Cure | Derive | Dissuade | Empathize |
| Curtail | Describe | Distinguish | Emphasize |
| Customize | Design | Distribute | Employ |
| Cut | Designate | Diversify | Enable |
| Dazzle | Detach | Divert | Enact |
| Debate | Detail | Divest | Encounter |

| | | | |
|---|---|---|---|
| Encourage | Excise | Fix | Guard |
| End | Excite | Focus | Guide |
| Endorse | Execute | Fold | Halt |
| Endow | Exercise | Follow | Halve |
| Energize | Exert | Forecast | Hammer |
| Enforce | Exhibit | Forewarn | Handle |
| Engage | Expand | Forge | Harness |
| Engender | Expedite | Forgive | Hasten |
| Engineer | Experiment | Form | Hear |
| Enhance | Explain | Formalize | Heighten |
| Enjoin | Explode | Formulate | Help |
| Enlarge | Exploit | Forward | Highlight |
| Enlist | Explore | Foster | Hire |
| Enliven | Export | Found | Hoist |
| Enrich | Expose | Frame | Hold |
| Enroll | Express | Freeze | Hone |
| Ensure | Expunge | Fulfill | Honor |
| Enter | Extend | Fund | Host |
| Entertain | Extract | Furnish | House |
| Entice | Extrapolate | Further | Hypothesize |
| Enumerate | Extricate | Fuse | Identify |
| Equate | Fabricate | Gain | Ignite |
| Equip | Facilitate | Garner | Illuminate |
| Eradicate | Factor | Gather | Illustrate |
| Erase | Familiarize | Gauge | Imagine |
| Erect | Fashion | Generate | Impart |
| Escalate | Feature | Ghostwrite | Impel |
| Escort | Feed | Give | Implement |
| Establish | Field | Glean | Import |
| Estimate | File | Govern | Impress |
| Evaluate | Fill | Grade | Improve |
| Evoke | Finagle | Graduate | Improvise |
| Examine | Finalize | Grant | Inaugurate |
| Excavate | Finance | Graph | Incite |
| Exceed | Find | Greet | Include |
| Excel | Finish | Groom | Incorporate |
| Exchange | Fit | Grow | Increase |

(continues)

**FIGURE 4-5. VERBS/ACTION WORDS.** (continued)

| | | | |
|---|---|---|---|
| Index | Iron | Mail | Navigate |
| Indict | Isolate | Maintain | Negotiate |
| Individualize | Issue | Make | Net |
| Induce | Itemize | Manage | Neutralize |
| Infer | Join | Maneuver | Nominate |
| Influence | Journalize | Manufacture | Normalize |
| Inform | Judge | Map | Notarize |
| Infuse | Justify | March | Note |
| Initiate | Kindle | Mark | Notify |
| Innovate | Knit | Market | Nudge |
| Inoculate | Label | Master | Number |
| Inspect | Land | Match | Nurture |
| Inspire | Landscape | Maximize | Observe |
| Install | Laud | Measure | Obtain |
| Instill | Launch | Mediate | Offer |
| Institute | Launder | Meet | Officiate |
| Instruct | Lead | Mend | Offset |
| Insure | Learn | Mentor | Open |
| Integrate | Lecture | Merge | Operate |
| Intensify | Legitimize | Mind | Optimize |
| Intercede | Lend | Minimize | Orchestrate |
| Intercept | Lessen | Mix | Order |
| Interest | Let | Mobilize | Organize |
| Interpret | License | Model | Orient |
| Interrogate | Lift | Moderate | Originate |
| Intervene | Lighten | Modernize | Outbid |
| Interview | Limit | Modify | Outdistance |
| Introduce | Link | Mold | Outdo |
| Invent | Liquidate | Monitor | Outmaneuver |
| Inventory | Listen | Motivate | Outpace |
| Invest | Litigate | Mount | Outperform |
| Investigate | Load | Move | Outrun |
| Invigorate | Lobby | Mow | Outsell |
| Invite | Locate | Multiply | Outsource |
| Invoice | Log | Name | Overcome |
| Involve | Magnify | Narrate | Overhaul |

| | | | |
|---|---|---|---|
| Overturn | Pledge | Prorate | Recall |
| Pack | Plow | Prosecute | Recast |
| Package | Poll | Prospect | Receive |
| Paint | Portray | Protect | Recite |
| Pair [couple] | Pose | Protest | Reclaim |
| Pamper | Position | Prove | Recognize |
| Paraphrase | Post | Provide | Recommend |
| Pare [cut] | Practice | Provoke | Reconcile |
| Part | Praise | Prune | Reconfigure |
| Participate in | Predict | Pry | Record |
| Partner with | Prepare | Publicize | Recover |
| Pass | Prescribe | Publish | Recruit |
| Patch | Present | Pull | Recycle |
| Patrol | Preserve | Pump | Redeploy |
| Pattern | Preside | Purchase | Redesign |
| Pause | Presort | Pursue | Reduce |
| Pay | Press | Push | Reengage |
| Peg | Prevail | Quadruple | Reengineer |
| Penalize | Prevent | Qualify | Refer |
| Penetrate | Print | Quantify | Reference |
| Perceive | Prioritize | Query | Refine |
| Perform | Probe | Question | Refocus |
| Permit | Process | Quicken | Reform |
| Persevere | Proclaim | Quiz | Reformat |
| Persuade | Proctor | Quote | Refresh |
| Phase | Procure | Raise | Refund |
| Photograph | Produce | Rally | Refute |
| Pick up | Profile | Rank | Regain |
| Pilot | Program | Rate | Regale |
| Pinpoint | Progress | Reach | Register |
| Pioneer | Project | React | Regulate |
| Pitch | Promise | Read | Rehabilitate |
| Place | Promote | Realize | Rehearse |
| Plan | Prompt | Reap | Reinstate |
| Plant | Proofread | Reassure | Reinvigorate |
| Play | Propel | Rebuild | Reject |
| Plead | Propose | Rebut | Relate |

(continues)

**FIGURE 4-5. VERBS/ACTION WORDS.** (continued)

| | | | |
|---|---|---|---|
| Relocate | Retrieve | See | Slash |
| Remand | Return | Segment | Slate |
| Remedy | Revamp | Seize | Slaughter |
| Remit | Reveal | Select | Smooth |
| Remodel | Reverse | Sell | Soften |
| Remove | Review | Send | Solder |
| Render | Revise | Separate | Solicit |
| Renegotiate | Revitalize | Sequence | Solidify |
| Renew | Revive | Serve | Solve |
| Renovate | Revolutionize | Service | Soothe |
| Reorganize | Reward | Set | Sort |
| Repair | Rewrite | Settle | Source |
| Replace | Risk | Sever | Spark |
| Replicate | Rivet | Sew | Speak |
| Reply | Rotate | Shape | Specialize |
| Report | Rouse | Share | Specify |
| Reposition | Route | Sharpen | Spin |
| Represent | Run | Shatter | Split |
| Reprimand | Safeguard | Shed | Sponsor |
| Reproduce | Salvage | Shelter | Spot |
| Request | Sanitize | Shelve | Spotlight |
| Require | Save | Shift | Spread |
| Rescind | Scan | Ship | Spur |
| Rescue | Schedule | Shlep | Stabilize |
| Research | Schlep | Shmooze | Staff |
| Reserve | Schmooze | Shop | Stage |
| Reshape | Scoop | Shorten | Standardize |
| Resist | Score | Shovel | Start |
| Resolve | Scour | Show | State |
| Respond | Scout | Showcase | Steer |
| Restore | Screen | Shrink | Stem |
| Restrict | Script | Shut | Stimulate |
| Restructure | Scrutinize | Shuttle | Stock |
| Retain | Seal | Sign | Stop |
| Retool | Search | Simplify | Streamline |
| Retrain | Secure | Sketch | Strengthen |

| | | | |
|---|---|---|---|
| Stretch | Tend | Tutor | Vindicate |
| Strip | Terminate | Type | Visit |
| Structure | Test | Unblock | Voice |
| Study | Testify | Uncover | Void |
| Submit | Thank | Underscore | Volunteer |
| Succeed | Theorize | Unearth | Vote |
| Sum | Thrive | Unify | Vow |
| Summarize | Tighten | Unite | Warn |
| Summon | Time | Unlock | Wash |
| Supersede | Top | Unpack | Watch |
| Supervise | Total | Unravel | Water |
| Supplement | Trace | Unveil | Weather |
| Supply | Track | Update | Weave |
| Support | Trade | Upend | Weigh |
| Surpass | Train | Upgrade | Welcome |
| Survey | Transact | Uphold | Weld |
| Suspend | Transcend | Upholster | Widen |
| Sustain | Transcribe | Up-sell | Win |
| Sway | Transfer | Urge | Wind |
| Sweep | Transform | Use | Wipe |
| Switch | Transition | Usher | Wire |
| Synthesize | Translate | Vacate | Withdraw |
| Systematize | Transmit | Validate | Withhold |
| Tabulate | Transport | Vary | Withstand |
| Tailor | Travel | Vault | Wow |
| Talk | Treat | Veer | Wrest |
| Tally | Trigger | Vend | Wring |
| Tap | Trim | Verify | Write |
| Target | Triple | Vest | Yield |
| Teach | Troubleshoot | Veto | |
| Tell | Turn | Vie | |
| Temper | Turn around | View | |

**VOLUNTEER EXPERIENCE SECTION**

Often overlooked or dismissed by candidates, volunteer experience is valuable information to a prospective employer if the skills used as a volunteer are relevant to an employer's requirements. For example, your volunteer work as a youth hockey coach is worth mentioning if you seek a paid teaching or coaching position, or any position requiring team-building skills. If hiring managers read of your service as a literacy tutor, they can easily infer your patience, a valuable skill. Likewise, if they see you participated in an AIDS charity bike ride from Boston to New York City, they can glean from this your goodwill, endurance, and determination, valuable skills in any organization.

**EDUCATION SECTION**

If you have completed one or more degrees, then include your graduation dates. Many employers interpret the absence of dates to mean candidates are (1) attempting to hide their age and (2) acknowledging that their age is something to be hidden. Why send these messages? Many talented, full-blown adults graduated from college before last Thursday. If you graduated in 1962, write it. Do you think the reader won't do the math some other way or won't figure it out when you meet? Don't hide your academic history. Write it proudly.

Many employers hiring recent graduates from MBA, JD, and some other programs require candidates to include their grade point average (GPA) on a résumé. Even if you are not a recent graduate, if you completed college or graduate school with a stellar GPA, you may choose to include it on your résumé. If you received honors, you may choose to include this information, too. If you attended school at night for four years, that says a lot about you, so there is no reason to keep it a secret, either:

**Education**
6/87–5/91          Clark University, Metropolis, MA (nights)
                   Bachelor of Science, Economics, GPA 3.59
[Strike the TAB key after the end date on the first line and at beginning of the second line.]

If still in school, write "degree expected [month/year]" after the name of the degree:

> **Education**
> 9/14–present          Clark University, Metropolis, MA
>                       Bachelor of Arts, Music, degree expected 5/18
> [Strike the TAB key after *present* on the first line and at beginning of the second line.]

If your résumé includes mention of a college degree (or "degree expected"), high school graduation is implied and thus need not be included.

If you have no college degree but some training, create a Relevant Coursework or Relevant Education/Training section (instead of an Education section) to include any relevant courses, seminars, or workshops you have completed, with the starting month and year (and ending month and year, if different) for each.

If you have no college education or relevant training but graduated from high school or earned your General Educational Development (GED), list it in your Education section. If you graduated from a specialized competitive-entry high school (for young artists or scientists, for example), specify this achievement.

If you have no material for an Education section, focus on writing the other sections where your self-taught skills will shine through (work experience, volunteer experience, software skills, language skills, and so forth) and increase your knowledge and marketable skills by taking useful courses online or at a school near you.*

### INVENTIONS, PUBLISHED WORKS, SEMINARS SECTION

If you have invented, published, or lectured, and if these accomplishments relate to your current career path, then include a section to briefly list them:

---

*An increasing number of schools and colleges now offer classes scheduled around the needs of working adults, both online and in person. Contact each school's financial aid office to learn how to get help with tuition, fees, books, childcare, and other expenses while you attend. Using your favorite search engine (e.g., *www.google.com*, *www.zoo.com*, or *www. duckduckgo.com*), be sure, too, to search for "MOOC" (without quotation marks) to learn about Massive Open Online Courses, available free at the time of this writing from a growing number of well-regarded institutions of higher learning.

**Published Works, Seminars**

| 9/01 | "Make Your Skills Jump off the Page" (seminar given at Metropolis University, Metropolis, NY) |
| 11/00 | "Résumés: Writing a Knock'em Dead Résumé" (article for ivillage.com) |
| 1/00 | "13 Truths About Résumés and Cover Letters" (article for writeresumesright.com) |

## SOFTWARE SKILLS SECTION

If you are not an information technology (IT) candidate, but you do use a personal computer (PC), then include on your résumé the operating systems (e.g., Windows, Apple iOS, Android, Chrome), office applications (e.g., Word, Excel, Access, PowerPoint, Publisher), and programming languages (e.g., HTML5, CSS3, C++, Java, Visual Basic, COBOL) you use. Refrain from including all version numbers; if you use one version, then you can learn another. Here is a sample:

**Software Skills**
Windows, Apple iOS, Word, Excel, PowerPoint, Publisher, Explorer

(This Software Skills section implies the ability to *use/navigate* Windows.)

Some candidates will include a long list of software skills on their résumé, then send their cover letter and résumé in a handwritten envelope. Learn to print an envelope. It will make your software claims a lot more credible.

The point of this section is not to list every application you have ever used. It is simply to convey two facts: (1) You do not fear technology and (2) faced with any new software, all you need is a user guide and a little time to master it.

If the speed and accuracy of your typing are impressive and the position you seek demands these skills, then take the test at *www.typingtest. com* (free at the time of this writing) and include the error-free result (e.g., "Word (80 wpm)") in this section.

If you are an IT candidate, you may naturally have a longer list of skills in this section. Use Software/Systems Skills (instead of Software Skills) as a heading, with subsections as needed:

**Software/Systems Skills**
**Languages/Environments:** PowerBuilder, Korn Shell, C, COBOL, Oracle SQLPlus, PL/SQL, Visual Basic, Visual InterDev (VB Script), CA-Librarian, CICS, TSO/ISPF, Focus, PL/1, MarkIV
**Operating Systems:** Unix AIX, MVS, DOS, Windows NT
**Databases:** Oracle, Access, ADR DataCom
**Desktop Applications:** Word, Excel, Adobe Dreamweaver 13.0, Explorer
**Machines:** IBM 370/158, IBM 3033, IBM 3083/Model B CPU, PCs

(This Software/Systems Skills section implies the ability to *program for* Windows.)

### LANGUAGE SKILLS SECTION

If you are fluent in any language other than English, include a Language Skills section on your résumé. Specify whether you read, write, and/or speak the language. For example:

**Language Skills**
Spanish (read), French (read, write, and speak), German (speak)

If you have mastered American Sign Language or Braille, include it in this section, too.

### MEMBERSHIPS SECTION

If your membership in an organization helps you build skills relevant to target employers, then include it.

If a membership (or volunteer experience) helps you effectively show-case marketable skills, then don't necessarily exclude it for fear of exposing other information. If, for example, you're actively involved in a group whose name reveals you may be lesbian, gay, bisexual, transgender, of a particular faith, or possess any other characteristic unrelated to merit—and if your role involves skills valuable to an employer—write it proudly. Being ruled out of a job on the basis of any criterion other than merit is a useful warning. You wouldn't want to work for such employers anyway. It's their loss. Many hiring managers with a brain and a pulse will happily scoop up qualified people to help them compete and win in the marketplace.

What do you do for the organization? Briefly mention it:

> **Memberships**
> 9/01–present          Gay and Straight Alliance of Xtown, Xtown, NY
> Co-facilitate 6 meetings (2 groups, 3 sessions each)/month. Contribute
> Web content.

When deciding to include or exclude, the test is this: Is the information needed to make an effective pitch? If, in this case, you have already included on your résumé plenty of other examples of group facilitation skills and Web writing experience, you may choose to omit this membership. Similarly, if you only attend groups (vs. co-facilitate them) and visit the website (vs. contribute content to it), then, again: Is the information needed to make an effective pitch?

In each case, use your judgment to assess the risks and benefits of inclusion. Do not prejudge all prospective employers as racist, homophobic, anti-faith, and so forth.

### REFERENCES STATEMENT?

Exclude "References available on request." Employers know this already.

### PERSONAL INFORMATION SECTION?

In the United States, listing one's age, height, and weight,* hobbies, interests, health, and marital or parental status on a résumé is generally a waste of the reader's time, and may be seen—depending on the organization's culture—as inappropriate, irrelevant, silly (not in the fun sense of the term), and of absolutely zero interest to the reader. Your résumé is not an autobiography.

Rather than omitting all hobbies and interests, however, you may decide there are exceptions. Use your judgment. If a particular hobby or interest genuinely contributes to your relevant skills, include it. If you choose to include a Relevant Hobbies/Interests section, proceed with caution.

---

*Unless one seeks an acting, modeling, physical education, or law enforcement job.

## ARTWORK, PHOTOS, DECORATIVE BORDERS, AND LINE ART

Artwork and photos are generally not part of a résumé. If they are required by an employer, include them in a separate portfolio.

Decorative borders and line art are similarly often inappropriate on a résumé. Fair or not, to many readers there is a fine line between artistic/whimsical (sometimes suitable) and flaky/inappropriate (at no time suitable). Skilled graphic artists know: Context is important. A résumé is generally not the proper context for decorative borders and line art.

Following on the next pages are four sample résumés using some of the previously mentioned résumé sections. Remember: The sequence, number, and nature of the sections you include on your résumé will be based not on any samples but solely on your unique story.

**Kyla Sample**
123 Main Street, Metropolis, NY 10001-0001
phone: 123-456-7890, fax: 234-567-8901, e-mail: kylasample@domainname.com

## Work Experience
10/05–present      Big Giant Company, Metropolis, NY
                   Director of Purchasing
Initiate sweeping vendor review and cut materials costs more than
$4.2M/year. Collaborate with sales, production, receiving, and suppliers
to implement just-in-time deliveries and eliminate $800K/year in
carrying costs. Renegotiate contracts and replace vendors to cut facility,
travel, technology, and supply costs $1.6M/year.

4/02–9/05          XYZ International, Metropolis, NY
                   Purchasing Manager
Launched, taught, and enforced purchase requisition system for use at
all levels to eliminate non-approved spending. Designed purchase order
forms to meet complex federal and international regulations. Developed
secondary suppliers for 100+ key materials to avoid sole sourcing.
Managed 8 staff. Served as Acting Director as needed.

7/96–2/02          ABC Inc., Metropolis, NY
5/99–2/02          Senior Buyer
7/96–4/99          Buyer

6/94–6/96          Little Tiny Company, Metropolis, NY
                   Assistant Buyer

## Volunteer Experience
3/03–present       Tutor, Literacy Volunteers of America, Metropolis, NY

## Education
9/97–5/99          Metropolis Business School, Metropolis, NY (nights)
                   Master of Business Administration

9/90–5/94          Metropolis University, Metropolis, NY
                   Bachelor of Science, Economics, *summa cum laude*

## Memberships
9/02–present       APICS, The Association for Operations Management
8/02–present       NAPM, Institute for Supply Management

## Software Skills
Windows, MAC-OS, Word, Excel, Publisher, Adobe Dreamweaver

## Language Skills
Read, write, and speak Spanish

## Jason Case
123 Main Street, Metropolis, NY 10001-0001
phone: 123-456-7890, fax: 234-567-8901, e-mail: jasoncase@domainname.com

### Education
9/14–present       MNO University, Metropolis, NY (eves/Saturdays)
                      Master of Social Work, degree expected 5/16

9/02–5/05        XYZ University, Metropolis, NY (nights)
                      Bachelor of Arts, Psychology, *magna cum laude*

9/00–5/02        ABC Community College, Metropolis, NY (nights)
                      Associate of Arts, Human Services Experience

### Experience
6/04–present      Metropolis Supported Housing, Metropolis, NY
                      Life Skills Counselor
Co-facilitate 5 weekly group therapy sessions. Contribute to 120+
treatment plans. Help public assistance recipients, ex-offenders, and
persons in substance abuse recovery improve communications skills,
manage anger, prevent conflict, and move to self-sufficiency. Advocate
for clients to get transitional benefits as they move to paid work.

12/02–5/04        Metropolis State Hospital, Metropolis, NY
                      Mental Health Aide
Helped 40+ clients with schizophrenia develop communications and
time management skills, hygiene, sound diet, and medication
compliance. Provided emotional support. Recorded observations for use
by clinicians. Supervised group recreational activities.

7/00–6/02        Metropolis Cares, Metropolis, NY
                      Community Outreach Worker
Created and delivered presentations to 100+ schools, hospitals, and
social service agencies. Grew client referrals 70% in 1 year. Co-
developed pitches to prospective donors. Recognized for contribution to
obtaining more than $1.6M in new donations.

### Memberships
5/04–present      American Counseling Association
5/01–present      American Mental Health Counseling Association

### Software Skills
Windows, Word, Excel, PowerPoint, Publisher, Adobe Dreamweaver

## Terri Example
123 Main Street, Metropolis, NY 10001-0001
phone: 123-456-7890, fax: 234-567-8901, e-mail: terriexample@domainname.com

**Goal**
Transition to and establish career in technical sales.

**Work Experience**
9/03–present        WidgetLand, Metropolis, NY
                    Assistant Network Administrator
Help maintain server, Internet/e-mail, and software to support 120-user local area network comprising human resources, sales/marketing, customer service, purchasing, accounting, and receiving/shipping applications. Train staff on sharing data among disciplines to improve performance in all areas. Initiate disaster plan to protect vital data.

12/02–present       Metropolis Technical College, Metropolis, NY
                    Technology Aide (part-time)
Support 600+ users of various skill levels on 40 PCs, 2 printers, 1 scanner, 1 fax, and 2 copiers. Help non-traditional students overcome fears of computing. Troubleshoot tech issues. Inventory supplies to prevent shortages. Select and install security software. Create popular "cheat sheets" for users to more easily navigate common applications.

**Volunteer Experience**
1997                Girl Scouts of America, Metropolis, NY
Recognized for achieving highest cookie sales in Metropolis.

**Education**
9/02–5/04           Metropolis Technical College, Metropolis, NY
                    Associate of Science, Computer Science

**Continuing Education**
3/05                Dale Carnegie Training, Metropolis, NY
                    How to Cold Call and Build New Customers

**Memberships**
1/04–present        Toastmasters International
12/02–present       Association for Computing Machinery

**Software/Systems Skills**
Windows NT, Novell, Word, Visual Basic, Access, Adobe Dreamweaver

## Miles Instance

123 Main Street, Metropolis, NY 10001-0001

phone: 123-456-7890, fax: 234-567-8901, e-mail: milesinstance@domainname.com

### Experience

9/04–present        MegaLoMart, Metropolis, NY
                    Customer Service Representative and
                    Front-End Supervisor

Manage cashiers, cash office, bridal registry, monogramming, and gift wrap services. Investigate and resolve customer inquiries on merchandise or service. Help hire and train 30+ staff. Awarded for managing highest volume sales ever during a single shift.

9/02–present        Shop and Get Out, Inc., Metropolis, NY (part-time)
                    Salesperson and Cashier, Accessories Department

6/01–8/01 and       Teeny Tiny Mart, Metropolis, NY
6/02–8/02           Cashier and Stock Clerk

### Education

9/14–present        Metropolis Business College, Metropolis, NY (nights)
                    Bachelor of Science, Business, degree expected 5/18

### Software Skills

Windows, Word, Excel, Adobe Dreamweaver

### Language Skills

Read, write, and speak Spanish

# FIVE

# Deliver Your Message the Right Way to the Right Places

Whether, how, when, and where to send your résumé are decisions as important as the decisions you make as you design each element of its content.

## SENDING YOUR RÉSUMÉ

Employers often receive résumés so unrelated to the requirements for an available position (and cover letters so devoid of enthusiasm) that they openly wonder why candidates even bothered to send them. This happens a lot.

Sending a résumé—no matter how well written—in response to an unsuitable opening is a common and easily preventable cause for receiving no invitation to interview. Ask yourself:

- Do I meet all or almost all requirements for the position?*
- Am I really interested in the work, hours, and location?

---

*In a job ad, the words *preferred, helpful, desirable*, and *a plus* do not mean "required." Sometimes, candidates confuse these terms and, as a result, miss out on many opportunities. Do not rule yourself out from responding to an ad because you don't have everything on an employer's wish list. Like everyone else, an employer may prefer lots of things. So what? Smart, caring, and enthusiastic candidates are easily trainable and often just what an employer needs. In the eyes of many hiring managers, these qualities easily outweigh the absence of one or two "preferred" items.

If either answer is no, then do not send your résumé. If both answers are yes, then respond to the ad or job listing by sending a Response Letter (see Chapter 6) and your résumé to the employer.

Unless specifically prohibited, send your documents every way you can, which includes by snail mail, fax, e-mail, and hand delivery. Repeated exposure shows perseverance and genuine interest.

Rather than sending your documents by all four methods at the same time, however, you may elect instead to wait a few days or even a week between methods to see in each case if fewer methods will generate a response. When you can, avoid snail mail as the first in your sequence, though, since it is the slowest of the four.* There's a fine line between perseverance and pestering; aim not to cross it.

Employers often receive e-mail attachments in file formats they cannot open. Such formats imply inconsiderate candidates. Do not assume employers have the time or the inclination to "unzip" or otherwise convert your files. E-mail your résumé either as a Microsoft Word (.doc or .docx file) or Adobe Reader (.pdf file) attachment** or in the body of an e-mail message. Doing so implies a considerate candidate.

If you send an attachment, first rename the file in a way that is helpful to the recipient. A file named "myresume" may be useful to you at home but is of little use to an employer receiving thousands of résumés. Instead, use an easily understandable naming protocol to name your file, like "resumelastnamefirstnamemonthdateyear" (e.g., "resumebennettscott08 0716" for a résumé submitted on August 7, 2016). (In the United States, month precedes date.) Doing so is a big help to the people receiving your information.

Although Microsoft Word (.doc or .docx file) or Adobe Reader (.pdf file) attachments are now generally accepted when sending e-mail, some

---

*When you do send snail mail, avoid using a postage meter. Using a meter may send two negative messages: 1) Rather than having been thoughtfully selected, the recipient is merely one of many in a mass mailing, and 2) you may inappropriately be using your current employer's postage meter, time, and other resources to find new work.

**Attaching your résumé to an e-mail message is a breeze. Using any e-mail program, click on COMPOSE or similar word and then look around for the word ATTACH (or the paper clip icon). Usually to the right of ATTACH, you will see a button marked BROWSE. Click on BROWSE, go to MY DOCUMENTS, double-click on your résumé, then—if your e-mail program requires it—click on OK or ATTACH.

employers require you instead to send your résumé in the body of an e-mail message. Here's how to do it.

### How to Send Your Résumé in the Body of an E-Mail

1. Using "Save As" in Microsoft Word, create a second version of your résumé in "text only" instead of "Word Document" format.
2. Remove italics, bold, and symbols, if any.
3. Delete tabs between text and replace them with one comma and one space.
4. "Align left" all text with a maximum of sixty-five characters and spaces per line.
5. Block (SHIFT-⇩) all text, copy (CTRL-C) it, and then paste (CTRL-V) it into the body of your e-mail.
6. Adjust it as needed in your e-mail.
7. E-mail it to yourself first. (Many candidates forget to do this.)
8. See how it looks on the screen when you receive it, and print it to see how it looks on paper.
9. Adjust it again as needed.
10. When your document looks great on screen and on paper, then block, copy, paste into a new e-mail, and send it to a prospective employer.

Responding to job listings—that is, sending a response letter and résumé—is not always the most effective way to find great work. See Chapter 6 to learn about the oft-forgotten yet powerful alternative, the Inquiry Letter.

Whether responding or inquiring, call—and check the website, if there is one—to obtain the correct spellings for the current names and titles of the human resources manager and the relevant department manager, even for names you are convinced have only one possible spelling.

### Applying Online

Many employers use online application systems. These vary in complexity from sites with a few simple fields followed by a straightforward way to attach a résumé, to mazelike sites that take seemingly forever to complete. The ease or complexity of a given site provides valuable insights into the employer's level of respect for prospective employees.

Completion of any such online application process is a personal decision for each candidate. If you elect to apply using any such site, I encourage you to create and maintain one consistent mechanism or storage location (e.g., a specific, well-named document in Notepad, which you'll find under Accessories; a specific, well-named draft message in a Gmail account you can set up at *www.gmail.com*; one safely stored piece of paper) to retain every username and corresponding password for every such site where you have applied. Such a mechanism or storage location prevents having to reenter all your information for each opening.

An interesting alternative for folks who chiefly fill out lots of repetitive paper and online job applications is *www.jobon.com,* a free site where candidates can conveniently provide information, including a brief video (webcam required) one time for many prospective employers to see.

### JOB/CAREER FAIRS AND REVERSE JOB/CAREER FAIRS

You may want to use your résumé at job/career fairs; proceed with caution when deciding whether to attend at all, however. The most successful such fairs (1) are free (beware if there is an admission fee), (2) include a substantial number of employers, and (3) are sponsored by a reputable organization.

Reverse job/career fairs, where candidates have booths and employers attend, are a recent phenomenon, and these too are best when they (1) are free to candidates, (2) include many employers, and (3) are sponsored by a trusted organization.

### RESPONDING TO BLIND ADS

Some ads do not reveal an employer or headhunter name. Why? There are many reasons. Here are three: A small employer may be trying to save money on an ad by reducing the number of words the ad contains. Another (less innocuous) reason is that a less-than-reputable headhunter may be trawling for résumés for potential employer-clients. A third reason is that an employer may not want to reveal a strategically important opening to suppliers, competitors, clients, or prospects.

Whatever the reason, there are several ways to look for the missing information. Here are two: If an ad lists only a fax number, go to *www.google.com*, *www.zoo.com*, or *www.duckduckgo.com*, and (1) type the fax number (e.g., "123-456-7890" with the quotation marks) and get the result or (2) type "freeality reverse lookup" and use the free tools there to get the result. If you find the result is a headhunter, you may choose not to respond. (Here's why: Reputable headhunters tend to proudly advertise their identities rather than hide them using blind ads.) However, you may find in the results an employer name and phone number. If so, you can call for the correctly spelled name of both the human resources manager and the hiring manager. Your response letter will be one of only a few in the stack with this information.

If an ad reveals only an e-mail address as the contact, there are many ways to find out more. Here are two: Usually, the part of the address after the @ sign is an active website address. Type it (the part after @) into your Web browser, get the results, and learn more. If the portion of the address after @ is a community or mail site (e.g., *www.gmail.com*, *www.yahoo.com*, *www.outlook.com*) rather than an employer website, then there's another way to learn more. Use *www.freeality.com* (or one of many other sites) to do a reverse lookup by e-mail address. Again, if you find the result is a headhunter, you may choose not to respond. However, you may find in the results an employer name and phone number. If so, you can call for the correctly spelled name of both the human resources manager and hiring manager. Again, your response letter will be one of only a few in the stack with this information.

If the ad contains only a post office box as contact, this is a giant red flag and you may not want to respond. Such ads may be from disreputable companies. However, if you decide to respond anyway, there is a way to learn more. Call the postal service in the city or town where the box is located. As of this writing, the postal service (in the U.S.) is required to disclose upon request the name of the owner of a post office box.

If the ad states only a newspaper's private box number as contact, this too may be a red flag. However, if you decide to respond anyway, there is little in this case you can do to discover the identity of the owner of the box unless you have a connection at the newspaper. Without asking anyone to break any rules, you can ask for the information, however, and a nice (or new) newspaper advertising department employee may provide it.

It is generally unwise to respond to requests for salary requirements (see Chapter 7) or salary history (again, see Chapter 7) when choosing to answer a blind ad. Giving such private data to an unnamed and unaccountable person or organization is an invitation to trouble.

If the job and the employer described in a blind ad strike you as familiar, if the ad reads like an upbeat version of your or a coworker's present job, then it may help to recall the famous horror movie line, "The call is coming from inside the house." Think about it.

## THINKING OUTSIDE THE CUBICLE

The extent to which you employ alternative formats and delivery methods for your content depends on the nature of the work you seek and where your target employer(s) spend(s) time. Consider form vs. function. Does the form undermine or sacrifice or divert attention from the function (i.e., your content, the pitch), or does it heighten and invigorate and propel active interest in it? Mindful of context, here are some alternatives. Proceed with caution.

| | |
|---|---|
| Billboard* | Newspaper front page |
| Board game | Nutrition label |
| Brochure/pamphlet | Paint can |
| Cereal box | Poem |
| Chocolate bar | Postcard |
| Cue card | Print ad (e.g., classified, mail order) |
| Handkerchief (e.g., "Don't blow it!") | QR (Quick Response) code** |
| Infographics (e.g., timelines, pie charts, bar graphs, Venn diagrams) | Short script or screenplay (genuinely short) |
| Jigsaw puzzle | Short story (genuinely short) |
| Measuring tape (e.g., résumé on one 60-inch line) | Street sign |
| Menu | Toolbox/toolkit |
| Movie poster | T-shirt |
| | Video |

*Less than $1,000 will, at the time of this writing, cover print/production/labor costs and rental expense for targeted, surplus (i.e., otherwise unsold) billboard space in many U.S. locations.

**Go to *www.google.com*, *www.zoo.com*, or *www.duckduckgo.com* and search "QR codes" for free sites where you can learn to create and read these codes. You may elect to use them to point prospective employers to a website where your résumé resides.

| | |
|---|---|
| Wanted poster | *www.google.com* result page |
| *www.amazon.com* product page | *www.linkedin.com* page format |
| *www.ebay.com* product page | *www.twitter.com* page format |
| *www.facebook.com* page format | |

Just when you thought the list of creative examples was finished . . . the following are examples of a variety of Internet sites (available at the time of this writing) that you can use as you see fit to creatively spread your content to prospective employers and beyond. Proceed with even more caution!

| | |
|---|---|
| *www.about.me* | *www.pulse.me* |
| *www.evernote.com* | *www.slideshare.net* |
| *www.facebook.com* | *www.snapchat.com* |
| *www.flickr.com* | *www.tumblr.com* |
| *www.flipboard.com* | *www.twitter.com* |
| *www.ghost.org* | *www.vimeo.com* |
| *www.instagram.com* | *www.vine.co* |
| *www.keek.com* | *www.visualcv.com* |
| *www.linkedin.com* | *www.wordpress.com* |
| *www.mobli.com* | *www.youtube.com* |
| *www.pinterest.com* | *www.zite.com* |

# SIX

# Cover Letters

You get only one chance to make a first impression. If you're like many candidates, you think it's when you walk into an interview, but it's really the moment a human resources or hiring manager glances at your cover letter. Few people will read even a perfect résumé if your cover letter has errors, is unclear, or is unfocused; and if in this case your résumé is left unread, there will be no in-person interview.

## COVER LETTERS IN GENERAL

In order to produce an error-free cover letter, be sure to remember these three items (excerpted here from the Introduction as reminders):

1. Don't count on your spell-check. Spell-check is not an editor: *form* vs. *from* escapes spell-check, as does *their* vs. *there* vs. *they're,* among countless other such examples. If one mistakenly types *copletion* instead of *completion,* several versions of Microsoft Word suggest replacing it with *copulation* instead of *completion.* Use a dictionary or my favorite free meta-dictionary site, *www.onelook.com.*

2. Don't skip the step of proofreading your finished product. In addition to rereading your documents from start to finish to check for clarity, also read them backwards to catch typos. This proven

technique will slow your reading and allow you to focus on each word.

3. Don't overlook having other qualified people review your finished product. Have your documents reviewed by at least two other people (a) who routinely hire people as part of their work and (b) whose writing skills and candor you respect. Here's the hard part: Listen to what they have to say. As writers, sometimes we have to delete cherished words and phrases to create the clearest, most focused documents. It often takes another qualified set of eyeballs to help us see this.

Unless there is a specific prohibition on phone calls stated in an ad or listing, call for the hiring manager's current title and the correct spelling of his or her name. If the organization is big enough, there will be both a human resources name and title and a hiring department manager name and title (obviously the same person if you seek a human resources position). Get both names—and send your letter to both—if you can. Ask to confirm the spelling even for names you think could have only one spelling. Chris could be Kris, Terry could be Terri, Mark could be Marc, John could be Jon, and Jason could be Jayson. Why not get noticed as the one in 100 candidates who took the time to get it right?

Make it easy for the reader to recognize and reach you. Block (SHIFT-⇩) and copy (CTRL-C) your "heading" (name, address, phone, fax, and e-mail) from your résumé and paste (CTRL-V) it at the top of your cover letter. Sometimes, cover letters mistakenly get separated from résumés. If a cover letter is compelling enough, it may even generate a phone call without a résumé, but only if contact information is on the letter.

If you use a similar letter for more than one employer, remember to change the name and address in each letter. Candidates reveal lack of attention to detail by leaving a wrong name or address in what looks like—because it is—a carelessly assembled form letter.

Less is more. A long cover letter is often interpreted to mean, "The following résumé may not be too clear, so here are the important things from it I'd like you to know." Is this an admission you want to make? Instead, have a clear and focused résumé so your cover letter need not be a novel. Your cover letter needs only to capture and express your enthusiasm, getting the reader to look at your résumé. Do not restate chunks of your résumé in your cover letter.

Anyone who advises candidates to write a four-paragraph cover letter is probably not an employer. You are more likely to win the lottery than to have any employer actually read a four-paragraph cover letter. Less really is more.

Beware of using humor. Professional comedians are paid well for a reason: Comedy is more difficult than it looks. Not only is comedy subjective (i.e., different people laugh at different things), but even one person will respond differently at different times to the same humor. Plus, there is the risk of unintentionally offending some readers. Overriding these issues, however, is the likelihood of appearing less than professional and, therefore, not being taken seriously as a candidate.

Have you ever written a sentence and then questioned yourself about its appropriateness? When this happens, it is a signal: Your instincts are telling you something. Listen to them. If you question the appropriateness of something you have written, your reader may, too. Trust your instincts and remove or replace the sentence.

Express your enthusiasm. If you don't feel it, stop writing and ask yourself: Is this simply a bad time to write, or am I genuinely not enthused about this employer? If the former is the case, write at another time. If the latter is true, do not bother to write the letter at all. You will save yourself and the employer valuable time.

As you write:

- Express your enthusiasm without false praise.
- Express confidence without arrogance.

These nuances are at the heart of a winning cover letter.

By the way, sign your letter. Do not use a hokey font that purports to—and never does—look like handwriting. However, if you use PC fax software to send your letter directly from Microsoft Word to the employer, then there is no paper to sign. Instead, (1) specify "Via fax software to: [fax number]" under the recipient's address and (2) leave no blank lines between "Respectfully," and your typed name. Similarly, you cannot (yet!) grab a pen and sign an e-mail message. You do not need to abandon the human touch completely, however. "Dear [Properly Spelled Contact Name]," and "Respectfully, [Your Name]" remain appropriate in e-mail messages to employers. Be one of the few people who help to prove that civility is not dead.

Figure 6-1 shows the text of a sample response letter for you to play with and make your own. Copying it word for word will prove embarrassing for you if competing candidates use the same text. Construct your letter to reflect your personality.

**FIGURE 6-1. SAMPLE RESPONSE LETTER**

**Jason D. Case**
123 Main Street, Metropolis, NY 10001-0001
phone: 123-456-7890, fax: 234-567-8901, e-mail: xyz@domainname.com

[Date]
Properly Spelled Contact Name
Properly Spelled Current Title
Properly Spelled Employer Organization Name
Properly Spelled Street Address
Properly Spelled City, ST nine-digit Zip code

Re: Title of Advertised Position

Dear [Contact Name],
   Given your requirements and my skills and experience, I may be the person you're after. I am enthusiastic about [Organization Name] and this work.
   Would you be so kind as to please review my résumé and contact me soon? I eagerly await your reply. Thank you in advance.

Respectfully,

Jason D. Case

Do you think this is too brief? If so, I ask you to stop thinking like a candidate and start thinking like an employer. Imagine you are an employer. You are slogging through (not actually reading) hundreds of four-paragraph and even page-long response letters. Suddenly, you come across a breezy four-line letter. It stands out from the stack. It is visually different. It reflects a reader who respects your time. This candidate's résumé is worth a look.

## THE UNSUNG HERO OF THE JOB SEARCH: THE INQUIRY LETTER

The inquiry letter is the unsung hero of the job search. It is arguably the least used and most powerful job search tool. Its use represents a very different way of looking for work. It changes the dynamic of the search, transitioning you to the role of an initiator from just one of many respondents.

New positions are frequently "in the pipeline"—being debated, created, and funded—well before a single job opening is posted. People are writing proposed job descriptions, fighting for budget dollars, and obtaining approvals for yet-to-be-advertised positions. A brief (!) enthusiastic inquiry letter and compelling résumé received during these planning stages often lead to a positive result for candidate and employer.

A well-written inquiry letter in a huge stack of response letters draws attention. Again, think like an employer: You're opening 100 response letters and one very different letter appears—it's oozing with enthusiasm, responding to nothing, from someone who just wants to be a part of your organization in whatever way you see fit. Wouldn't that letter stand out from the stack? Of course, it would. It's always refreshing to see the initiative and genuine interest an inquiry letter represents.

Figure 6-2 shows the text of a sample inquiry letter for you to play with and make your own. Copying it verbatim will prove embarrassing for you if competing candidates use the same text. Write your letter to reflect your personality.

You may choose to include (briefly!) why you're interested. For example:

- I would like very much to be a part of X Hospital, the place that helped me deliver three of my children—now adults—into the world.
- A loyal subscriber for 10 years, I would like very much to be a part of X Magazine.

**FIGURE 6-2. SAMPLE INQUIRY LETTER**

**Kyla M. Sample**
123 Main Street, Metropolis, NY 10001-0001
phone: 123-456-7890, fax: 234-567-8901, e-mail: xyz@domainname.com

[Date]

Properly Spelled Contact Name
Properly Spelled Current Title
Properly Spelled Employer Organization Name
Properly Spelled Street Address
Properly Spelled City, ST nine-digit Zip code

Dear [Contact Name],

Do you have or expect any open X positions in your organization that can make use of my skills and experience? I would like very much to be a part of [Organization Name]; I decided the best way to accomplish this is to ask you directly.

Would you be so kind as to please review my résumé and contact me soon? If you have no X positions available now or in the pipeline, but will point me toward other possibilities, I'd sure appreciate that, too. I eagerly await your reply. Thank you in advance.

Respectfully,

Kyla M. Sample

## INFORMATIONAL INTERVIEW REQUEST LETTER

Career path reconnaissance on the Web and at the library can yield much useful information, but even after you've read all you can about a line of work, you may still have unanswered questions. It is often helpful to meet with an expert in your field of interest. An experienced perspective is invaluable.

Identify, ask, and meet with experts. Thorough career path reconnaissance can provide you with the names of experts in your field of interest. Send an informational interview request letter to several experts near you. There are many busy and well-paid experts kind and generous enough to allocate 30 minutes *pro bono* to help a newcomer.

Do not abuse this generosity by exceeding the allotted time or seeking a job from the expert. Instead, use the time to (1) ask thoughtful questions prepared in advance, (2) listen carefully to the answers (some of which may generate added or revised questions), and (3) take notes. Your *only* goal at an informational interview is to gain insights into the field. An expert may also provide you with contacts in a position to help you secure a position, but this is certainly not required—so do not expect it. Plus, if you attempt mid-meeting to change the stated agenda and cajole job leads from the expert, you risk creating a powerful foe and developing a poor reputation in your new field of interest.

**FIGURE 6-3. SAMPLE INFORMATIONAL INTERVIEW REQUEST LETTER**

**Miles J. Instance**
123 Main Street, Metropolis, NY 10001-0001
phone: 123-456-7890, fax: 234-567-8901, e-mail: xyz@domainname.com

[Date]

Properly Spelled Contact Name
Properly Spelled Current Title
Properly Spelled Employer Organization Name
Properly Spelled Street Address
Properly Spelled City, ST nine-digit Zip code

Re: Request for an Informational Interview

Dear [Contact Name],

   I seek to learn more about transitioning to a career in X. I have read about X in *The U.S. Occupational Outlook Handbook* and other places, and yet I realize there is no substitute for experience. My reconnaissance tells me you're an expert.

   Would you be so kind as to meet with me for 30 minutes at a date and time convenient for you so I may ask you some prepared questions? I'd be very grateful. If your schedule does not permit this, would you kindly refer me to a suitable colleague? Thank you in advance.

Respectfully,

Miles J. Instance

P.S. I enclose my résumé as an introduction and to give you a sense of my skills.

Learn all you can about the field before you meet the expert. Otherwise, you will be wasting his or her (and your) time on questions easily answered on the Web or at the library.

Prepare your written questions before you send an informational interview request letter, because the letter may quickly yield an unexpected phone call from the expert offering to answer questions on the phone. Be ready.

Figure 6-3 shows the text of a sample informational interview request letter for you to play with and make your own. Do not copy it verbatim. Again, craft your letter to reflect your personality.

Error-free, clear, and focused cover letters are engaging, persuasive, powerful, and rare. You now have the information you need to craft yours.

# SEVEN

# The Final Three Pre-Interview Items: Salary Requirements, Salary History, References

Here's how you can prepare thoughtful responses to requests for salary requirements, salary history, and references—items for which on-the-fly answers will not suffice.

## REQUEST FOR SALARY REQUIREMENTS

Employers request salary requirements for several important reasons. Here are three:

1. They don't have time to interview people they can't afford to hire.
2. They don't want to waste the time of candidates they can't afford to hire. It's a small world: An applicant today may be a valued client or supplier or employer tomorrow.
3. They want to see if the candidate can follow directions. This is the reason few people talk about. Employers want to see if a prospective employee will do as asked, rather than ignore a request simply because the task—in this case, writing a thoughtful answer—is challenging. This is why many employers discard response letters and résumés from people who fail to address this request.

Here's a sample response. Place your version at the end of your response letter.

> P.S. While I also place value on a number of other factors, I require a starting salary in the mid-$80s [or low $Xs, mid-$Xs, high $Xs].

On the phone or in person, if asked about these "other factors," include location, benefits, hours, working environment, company culture, opportunity for advancement, and any other noncash items of genuine importance to you. Although it's not required, you may also choose to include some of these items in parentheses after the word *factors* and before the comma in the sample given.

Notice that ranges are used, not specific numbers. This gives the hiring manager an opportunity to exercise judgment and shows your flexibility as well.

Do not include a statement of salary requirements unless an employer first requests one. Doing so (1) is usually seen as inappropriate, (2) may remove you from consideration, (3) reveals too much information, and (4) may cost you money if the budgeted range for the position is above your stated requirements.

## What if an employer reads my salary requirements and then ignores my résumé?

If this happens, then you are not a match for the current position, and your candor will have saved both you and the employer a lot of time and energy. Plus, smart employers review and set aside rather than ignore or shred the résumé of a skilled candidate they can't afford now; when a different position or more funding emerges, the candidate may be the perfect match.

### REQUEST FOR SALARY HISTORY

Many candidates are annoyed by a request for salary history, and with good reason. Yes, it's intrusive. Yes, it's a red flag. Based on such a request, you may decide that the requesting organization is not the right employer for you. A request for salary history is the sign of an employer who mistakenly thinks there is some connection between previous and desired salaries. Such requests reflect a narrow view of the world and fail to recognize that (1) some people will gladly take a pay cut for the right position and (2) some people may have been significantly underpaid in the past and have no intention of continuing to be underpaid.

In any case, candidates risk having their response letters and résumés discarded by not responding to the request. Figure 7-1 is a sample salary history. Only provide a salary history if it is requested.

Notice the absence of the starting month and year and ending month and year to the left of each employer's name. Unlike on a résumé, where such information is of use to the reader, it adds no value here and so can be excluded. Such dates to the left of each title are of use and important to include. Notice, too, **boldface** may be used as shown to direct reader's attention *if* more than one current position, especially if the positions are not adjacent to each other on the list.

In the United States, an Equifax-owned company, *www.thework number.com*, reportedly collects and sells the detailed employment and salary histories of an ever-increasing number of people to prospective employers, landlords, lenders, and more. Learn more, and protect your rights: (1) Go to *www.consumer.ftc.gov* and read all about the Fair Credit Reporting Act and how to get genuinely free annual credit reports (while avoiding look-alike scams), (2) review your information carefully, and (3) have any and all errors corrected.

## ELEMENTS OF COMPENSATION FOR SALARY HISTORY

Use the final (not the starting) compensation number for each position. Compensation includes more than salary. Remember to include:

- Differentials for work locations or shift schedules
- Overtime pay (which many candidates forget to include)
- Monetary value of compensatory (comp) time
- Bonuses
- Commissions
- Stock options
- Employer contributions to retirement plans
- The annual monetary value of extraordinary benefits:
  - Portion of paid time off ("PTO") or vacation above industry standard

FIGURE 7-1.

| Scott A. Bennett<br>Confidential Salary History | |
| --- | --- |
| **Employer** | **Final Compensation** |
| writeresumesright.com, Metropolis, CT | |
| 1/00–**present**  General Manager (part-time) | variable |
| | |
| ABC-Metropolis Psychiatric Hospital, Metropolis, CT | |
| 3/11–3/14  Licensed Clinical Social Worker II | $100,000 |
| 1/08–3/11  Licensed Clinical Social Worker | $70,000 |
| | |
| ABC University School of Medicine, Dept. of Psychiatry, Metropolis, CT | |
| 7/05–6/07  Post-MSW Fellow, Clinical Social Work | $19,000 |
| | |
| XYZ Foundation, Metropolis, NY | |
| 9/00–3/01  Career Developer | $45,000 |
| | |
| ABC College School of Business, Metropolis, NY | |
| 11/97–5/99  Career Services Counselor | $36,000 |
| | |
| Self-employed, Metropolis, NY | |
| 5/96–**present**  Freelance Writer and Lecturer | variable |
| | |
| FireSoft/Public Service Computer Software, Inc., Metropolis, MA | |
| 8/94–4/96  President/Chief Operating Officer | $120,000 |
| 6/93–8/94  Sales and Marketing VP | $80,000 |
| 4/92–6/93  Sales Manager | $40,000 |
| | |
| Tulip/Polymerics, Inc., Metropolis, MA and Cityville, MA | |
| 10/90–4/92  Director of Purchasing | $67,000 |
| | |
| Command Marketing/American Optical Corporation, Metropolis, CA | |
| 4/89–7/90  Manager, Materials and Distribution | $42,000 |
| 1/87–4/89  Materials Project Manager | $35,000 |
| 1/86–1/87  Manager, Distribution, Western U.S. | $28,000 |
| | |
| MetPath, Inc., Metropolis, CA and Eville, CA | |
| 1/85–1/86  Operations Manager | $24,000 |
| 9/84–1/86  District Logistics Manager | $22,000 |
| 9/83–9/84  Logistics Manager | $18,000 |
| 6/83–9/83  Medical Courier | $12,000 |

- 24/7 use of company vehicle
- Housing allowance
- 100 percent tuition assistance
- 100 percent health/disability/life insurance coverage with no paycheck deduction
- Health club membership
- Childcare services
- Concierge services
- Parking space in locations where parking is scarce (in several U.S. cities, this benefit is worth from $2,400 to over $7,000 per year, at the time of this writing)

Plus, if you declined to participate in an employer's health insurance plan because, for example, you were already covered under your spouse's/partner's plan, then the employer may have paid you a share of the resulting savings. If so, then these payments are part of your compensation, too.

## REFERENCES

A very popular reason employers request references is to see if a candidate is dumb enough to give bad ones. Few people talk about this, but now you know it. It's so easy to get this right, yet many candidates get it wrong.

Ask potential references before using them as references. Many candidates forget to do this, and people (even people who could have been excellent references) don't like such surprises. Prospective employers cannot always discern (nor should they have to) the difference between (1) the irritated voice of an unhappily surprised person and (2) a genuinely unenthusiastic reference.

Are you unsure how to ask someone to be a reference? If so, here are two ways:

1. "Are you willing to serve as a reference for me?"
2. "May I include your name and number when I provide references to employers?"

However you ask, after you ask, stop talking. Listen carefully to the response. Listen to both the content and the tone of the response. If a potential reference's response is anything other than genuinely enthusiastic, do not use that person as a reference.

If a potential reference respects your work but performs poorly on the phone, proceed with caution. A prospective employer—or anyone else, for that matter—can easily confuse a naturally low-key or monotone voice with an absence of enthusiasm. Smart candidates prevent this confusion whenever possible. Follow your instincts. You may choose not to use the person as a reference, or you may simply warn prospective employers. For example, "Please bear in mind when you call her that Georgette is quite soft-spoken, but she has consistently rated my work 'outstanding' on performance appraisals."

Figure 7-2 is a sample. Provide such data only if it is requested.

FIGURE 7-2.

### Scott A. Bennett
### Professional References

Please contact only in the event I am a finalist. Thank you in advance for your discretion.

John Lennon, VP, Operations (direct report)
ABC-Metropolis Psychiatric Hospital, Metropolis, CT
123-456-7890 (office)

Paul McCartney, Director of Student Services (final direct report)
ABC College School of Business, Metropolis, NY
234-567-8901 (office)

George Harrison, PhD (professor, professional ethics)
Professor, Counseling Psychology Program
Metropolis University/Downtown Campus, Metropolis, NY
345-678-9012 (office)

Ringo Starr, EdD (professor, group counseling)
Adjunct Professor, Counseling Psychology Programs, Retired
Metropolis University/Uptown Campus, Metropolis, NY
456-789-0123 (home)

Limit references to persons for whom you have completed paid or volunteer or academic assignments.

It's helpful to prospective employers to know with whom they are speaking: Is it your manager ("direct report")? An instructor? After each name, explain the reference's relationship to you.

Be sure you are using the current phone number and only the one specified (office, home, or cell) by each reference.

Candidates whose work experience is with a family business face a special challenge. Although such references may understandably be viewed as less credible, include a relative as a reference if you worked for an extended period for the person. Explain the situation to each prospective employer requiring references.

———

We've examined the ways you can market your skills and experiences to employers. Next, let's look at how you market to *yourself*.

# EIGHT

# Marketing to Yourself

Many career writers often use the term "market yourself." Words matter, though, so let's clarify. What they really mean is "market your skills and experience," not "market yourself."

Another popular phrase used by career writers discussing salary is, "What are you worth?" Again, words have meaning, and clarity is excellence. These writers really mean, "What are some employers paying for a specific set of skills and experience?"

Why are these distinctions important? Because inaccurate but commonly used phrases such as these feed into the crazy and widely held notion that "I am my work." If you believe you are your work, then what are you when you are out of work?

"I am my work" is just one example of the many crazy ideas we quietly tell ourselves again and again for years. What we tell ourselves—that is, how we market *to* ourselves—is at least as important as how we market our skills and experience to employers.

If you believe you can't find work, you are likely to construct a résumé and do other things that reinforce your belief. Few people do things in opposition to their own beliefs. Do you recognize any of this thinking?

- I am my work.
- Without my work I am nothing.
- I can't find work.

- I'm too young for any employer to hire me.
- I'm too old for any employer to hire me.
- I'm too old to start a new career.
- If I were a minority, I would get the job.
- If I were a white male, I would get the job.
- If I were taller, I would get the job.
- I'm underqualified.
- I'm overqualified.
- Most of the jobs out there are beneath me.
- Employers feel threatened by my skills and experience.
- Employers think former entrepreneurs can't work for others.
- I was fired, and I'll never find another job.
- I was laid off, and I'll never find another job.
- I resigned, and I'll never find another job.
- Employers don't understand the duties of a working parent.
- I've sent out lots of résumés and had no luck. See?
- It's political. It's who you know, not what you know.
- The longer it takes, the less likely I will ever find a job.
- There are no jobs out there for me.
- Each day I remain unemployed proves I can't find another job.
- My search efforts shouldn't have to be like a full-time job.
- I should already have the job and salary I want.
- Employers should respond to my résumé.
- If I do not get a response from Company X, it will be awful.
- An employer must call me this week.
- If I don't get a job this week, it will be awful. I can't stand it.

None of these beliefs really serves the believer. Think about your beliefs about yourself, others, and the world. How are these beliefs working out for you?

How we react to and handle events is determined not by the events themselves but by how we view the events, often through the prism of our deeply held irrational beliefs. Although humans have a natural tendency to collect and nurture wacky beliefs, we also have the capacity to identify, examine, and replace those wacky beliefs with effective rational beliefs.

For more information, read *A Guide to Rational Living* by Albert Ellis and Robert Harper (North Hollywood, CA: Wilshire Books, 1998).

# NINE

# Bonus Interview Chapter, by Popular Demand:

## Scott, My Résumé Worked! Now What?!*

You sent out your cover letter and résumé just the other day . . . and already, a voice mail message arrives, or an e-mail comes in: Your cover letter and résumé have successfully propelled active interest from a targeted employer! What next?

1. I challenge you to give credit where credit is due. Please join me in congratulating you on your effective cover letter and résumé. If you mistakenly believe receiving invitation(s) to interview is on account of luck, allow me to set the record straight. Your error-free, clear, focused, and targeted cover letter and résumé made your good luck. Again, congratulations!
2. Please take a few moments to send a message about your success to me at bennettcenterllc@gmail.com. Few things satisfy like seeing merit and hard work rewarded. I will not rent, nor will I sell, your e-mail address to anyone, ever. I do, however, reserve the right to do my Happy Dance in your honor.
3. Now, with the following tips for an effective interview, go make some more luck!

---

*Pre-interview preparation/position-specific interview training from some employers is, at the time of this writing, available free online from *www.learnup.com*. This service helps entry-level candidates prepare and then apply for relevant openings.

A job interview is a two-way process. Each participant is learning about the other in order to gather enough information to make a sound decision. Awareness of this fact commonly helps candidates reduce distress and increase focus, in advance of and during and after each interview.

A big unwritten—until now, that is—secret: Far and away, the most common reason candidates get the interview and not the job is . . . they're in the wrong place. Their cover letter and résumé generated a response from an employer who is not a fit. Please bear in mind, "not a fit" does not mean "evil employer" or "poor candidate" or "bad luck"—even though many candidates cling to these and other mistaken conclusions.

Instead: (1) Revisit the targeting that generated such interviews: Are your cover letters and résumé going to the right places? (2) Upon further reflection, are any employers a target chiefly or wholly because someone else thinks they should be? (3) Are you now willing to give increased and sustained attention to each employer's requirements—even if it leads to fewer items sent each day? (4) Adapt, exhibit flexibility, be nimble, and "grab the wheel" to take—or take back—control of your active career search.

**PHYSICAL PREP**

- Dress appropriately. If unsure, ask a trusted source.
- Use no perfume or cologne or scented body spray. Allergies are common.
- Minimize jewelry, unless context permits (e.g., art gallery, jeweler, fashion designer).
- Expose no or few tattoos or piercings, unless context permits.
- Wear no Bluetooth device or earphones on or about the head or neck or elsewhere.
- Bring a watch. Do not use a cell phone to check the time during a job interview.
- If you're driving to the interview location, is your vehicle clean, inside and out? You may be asked without warning to drive one or more people someplace (e.g., to an off-site interview or facility tour or luncheon).
- Bring a small tote with some facial tissue, a hand towel, dental floss, mini nail clipper, detergent stick/wipe, breath mints, a comb or brush as needed, two suitable pens, and one suitable notebook.

- Allow plenty of extra time for traffic, parking, and unexpected delays. Arrive early enough to allow time to visit a restroom before the interview to:
  - Check your nose. (Got tissue?)
  - Check your teeth. (Got floss?)
  - Check your fingernails. (Got mini nail clipper?)
  - Check your hair. (Got comb or brush?)
  - Check your shirt or blouse, tie, fly/pants or skirt or dress, and shoes. (Got a detergent stick/wipe?)
- Expel any tobacco, chewing gum, jerky, licorice whips, toothpicks, or other like items.
- Use a breath mint as needed. (Got breath mints?)
- Turn your cell phone completely off.
- Turn your cell phone completely off.
- Turn your cell phone completely off.
- If you have chronically wet hands, then grab some paper towels. (If none are available: Got hand towel?) Bring paper towels or a hand towel with you to the interview, and openly use either, as needed, immediately before shaking hands. A soggy handshake is a near-certain job-killer.

## MENTAL PREP

Physical prep is important—and mental prep is, too.

### Take Advantage of the Facial Feedback Hypothesis

Psychologists have long theorized that smiling can genuinely help a person feel happy. If you are feeling down as you enter a job interview, nearly any skilled interviewer can easily detect it. Contempt or weariness or frustration is often not nearly as well disguised as one may have hoped. If we smile for a solid minute or so (ideally, begin a few moments before entering the interview), the theory holds that we activate neurotransmitters that make us feel happy. We're not aiming for euphoria here, merely sufficient perkiness for a positive job interview. If you're feeling blue, then smile—a nice big grin, for a solid minute or so—and see for yourself.

## Take Advantage of the Halo Effect

When we observe one good thing about someone new to us, we assume all kinds of other good things about the person. It's not fair, but we do it anyway. For example, if you're a snappy dresser, some interviewers will assume you are more likely a responsible person in other, more important ways, too—even if, in fact, you are not. This means that for each thing you are seen doing well, more good things are assumed!

## Watch Out for the Fundamental Attribution Error

If you're having lunch with your best friend and see surplus spinach lodged between his teeth, you may very well point to the trouble spot as you hand him a piece of your floss stash, he uses it as indicated, and you both continue your lovely conversation without missing a beat. On the other hand, what if you were meeting him for the first time and saw him with spinach stuck between his teeth? You may readily think he's a spinach-lodged-in-the-teeth kind of guy generally. We tend to attribute a stranger's behavior to his disposition rather than to the situation. This is known as the fundamental attribution error, and examples of it are plopped all over every job interview where we've only just met the interviewer for the first time. It's not fair, and yet now that you're aware of it, you can see the value in taking a few moments to do your physical preparations and help prevent mistaken impressions.

## Tend to the Three Goals of Interpersonal Effectiveness

Seattle psychologist Marsha Linehan proposed—and I now paraphrase—inviting into our awareness three goals as we engage in any interaction: Maximize the chances of (1) getting what we want, (2) nurturing the relationship, and (3) nurturing self-respect. I encourage you to view each interaction in your career search—written or spoken—with these three goals in mind. Each of the three goals will not always get $33^{1}/_{3}$ percent of your focus, depending on the context of your interaction, and that's okay. The three are not listed in order of importance; that's up to you. Simply allowing all three goals into your awareness will put you ahead of many, if not most, candidates.

## READ UP AND THEN MEET UP

Before you work with a headhunter, get a copy of this must-read: *Rites of Passage at $100,000 to $1 Million+: Your Insider's Lifetime Guide to Executive Job-Changing and Faster Career Progress in the 21st Century* by John Lucht (Raleigh, NC: Viceroy Press, 2001). Among other things, Lucht explains the differences between contingency and retainer headhunters and hybrids of both, and he provides detailed strategies for dealing with each type.

Before your next interview, buy and read *How to Win Friends and Influence People* by Dale Carnegie, a timeless classic since 1936, available in paperback or on audio if you prefer. If you are open to the idea of improving your interpersonal skills, this can be a life-changing book.

If you seek a management position—any management position—then read *Quality Is Free: The Art of Making Quality Certain* by Philip Crosby (1980). Apply the author's ideas to any industry (really) and you will delight customers. People who read it carefully are usually guided by its principles forever. Many interviewers love candidates with a genuine understanding of this subject.

Do all of your face-to-face interactions—in-flight, in traffic, with parking attendants, security guards, fellow elevator travelers, secretaries, HR staff, and other potential colleagues—convey the same level of courtesy and respect as your interactions with the hiring manager(s)?

I'm not the only hiring manager to routinely ask colleagues for their impressions of each candidate I interview . . . and, on more than a few occasions, my colleagues have saved me from being played by an otherwise-compelling candidate who, I later learned, extended courtesy and kindness only to me. Generally—like so many other humans—smart employers want to work/spend time with people whose courtesy and kindness are genuine rather than a façade.

## ARE YOU READY FOR YOUR CLOSE-UP?

Dress well, flash your most winning smile, and remember to sit in front of your most impressive wall. Chances are rapidly increasing for active career seekers to be invited to engage in long-distance remote interviews using sites like *www.skype.com* or *www.google.com/hangouts* or *www.tango.me* or *www.viber.com* or *www.zoom.us*. More and more employers find remote video interviews allow them to "meet" with faraway candidates quasi-face-to-face while saving time and money. If your device is connected to reliably speedy Internet access and equipped with working webcam, microphone, and speakers, then you're ready to go. Be patient with all participants; using some of these services is a bit like watching TV in 1948—the technology, while improving, is still a work in progress. Just like your e-mail address and your outgoing voice mail message, your Skype name ought to be serious rather than silly. Avoid using any name that could keep you from being taken seriously by prospective employers.

Whether a job interview is 1:1 or with a panel/hiring committee, whether its style is casual, structured, semistructured, or an intentional "stress" interview, whether on-site or off-site, seated or walking, by phone, audio-only conference call, 1:1 video phone, or video conference call, project the best "you" that you can be.

**FIGURE 9-1. PUTTING YOUR BEST FOOT FORWARD.**

| Smart employers hire the candidate most likely to . . . | How you can prove it's you: |
|---|---|
| . . . not someday steal their resources to find another job. | Don't use work resources (e.g., phone numbers, postage meter) in your job search. |
| . . . follow instructions. | If a posting says no phone calls, don't call; if it asks for salary history and/or requirements, provide the requested information. |
| . . . write well. | Create an error-free, clear, focused, and compelling cover letter and résumé. |

| . . . respect deadlines. | Be on time. Train, plane, and automobile traffic delays are not the employer's problem. Leave plenty of extra time. |
| . . . be a nice person. | Be genuinely friendly with the security guard, the secretary, and not just the boss. |
| . . . be honest. | Don't make stuff up. |
| . . . actively listen to others. | Focus more attention on what the interviewer is saying and less on what you'll say next. Pause briefly (i.e., a few seconds) after the interviewer has spoken. |
| . . . actively listen to others! | Does each of your answers address the question asked, and only the question asked? |
| . . . speak well. | Avoid using "um," "ah," "like," "you know," "okay," "gonna," and slang generally. |
| . . . present well. | Dress appropriately. If in doubt about an item, wear something else. |
| . . . be genuinely enthusiastic. | Use direct eye contact. (In the United States, lowering one's gaze is usually viewed as meekness rather than respect.) Think about the great opportunity here. |
| . . . not bad-mouth them in the future. | Do not speak poorly of a current or former employer. As Father Divine (c. 1876–1965) preached, "Accentuate the positive." |
| . . . know what s/he doesn't know (one sure sign of a smart person). | Ask relevant questions. Give examples of when you've turned to others for help. |

(continues)

**FIGURE 9-1. PUTTING YOUR BEST FOOT FORWARD.** (continued)

| | |
|---|---|
| . . . know who s/he is and where s/he's going. | When asked, "Tell me about yourself," have ready a compelling two-minute answer consisting of three parts, around 40 seconds each: (1) where you've been, (2) where you're going, and (3) precisely why you're now sitting across from this interviewer in this organization. |
| . . . think before s/he speaks. | Think before you answer. A brief pause to reflect upon a question and consider your response is perfectly appropriate. |
| . . . think before s/he speaks! | Think before you ask. Is your question relevant, well-timed, and something that hasn't already been answered? |
| . . . know something about their organization. | Enthusiastically plop some nonobvious printed research on the interviewer's desk while restating your interest and excitement. |
| . . . know the organization's mission and relevant trends. | Include in your research external articles on important, relevant news and trends. |
| . . . prioritize, plan, and organize well. | Answer complex, multipart questions thoughtfully yet concisely. |
| . . . think rationally and have analytical skill. | Give a specific example illustrating how you solved a complex and challenging problem |
| . . . not avoid or disdain constructive criticism. | Provide an example of when you proactively sought and gratefully received criticism and rapidly applied the lesson(s) learned. |
| . . . know his/her job is one part of the whole, one aspect of the big picture. | Express interest in the entire organization and ask how your (!) role will (!) fit into it. |

| | |
|---|---|
| . . . get along with others and be able to work as part of a team. | Give a specific example from work, school, or volunteer activities, ideally, of how you've (1) worked with people with a variety of personalities and levels of skill, interest, and motivation and (2) proactively shared the credit for successful outcomes. |
| . . . question the status quo and innovate. | Share an example demonstrating your ability to achieve positive change (e.g., cut costs, grow sales, measurably improve quality of customer experience) by introducing a new idea and bringing others on board to make it happen. |
| . . . be at ease with technological changes. | State that with a user guide and a couple of days, you'll figure out their software. |
| . . . effectively manage projects and processes. | Give a specific example from work, school, or volunteer activities. |
| . . . make decisions and solve problems. | Give a specific example from work, school, or volunteer activities. |
| . . . manage relationships. | Give a specific example from work, school, or volunteer activities. |
| . . . manage across disciplines. | If you haven't, be sure to mention specific, relevant, and readily transferable skills you can bring to bear to allow you to do so. |

Think through, create, and then practice at least 100 times in front of a mirror your most compelling 60- to 90-second response to the very predictable question, "Why should I/we hire you?" If you focus the content of your response entirely on what's in it for the employer and not what's in it for you, then you will stand apart from most candidates.

Think about, develop, and then practice at least 100 times in front of a mirror an honest 60- to 90-second response to, "Tell me about one weakness/one area where you see room for growth/room for improvement." Instead of using common and painfully obvious dodges like "I'm

a perfectionist" or "I work way too hard," prepare and rehearse a genuine response. Select something real and then do not neglect to mention in
your reply the specific, ongoing actions you are taking to achieve mastery
in the area you selected. An honest answer to this routine question reflects
self-awareness and humility, two traits generally prized in the job market.

I encourage you too to "take the temperature" of each interviewer,
and by this I mean, before the exit handshake, directly ask questions like,
"Can you envision me in this position?" and "Am I competing with dozens of other candidates, or a handful, or . . . ?" After each question, it is
crucial for you to stop talking and actively listen, with eyes and ears, to
the answers.

Unless you are given the information without asking for it, do not
leave any job interview without asking directly, "Where are you now in
your process?" Getting a sense of what stage of the hiring process the
employer is in before leaving your interview helps you develop an effective post-interview strategy.

Remember too to ask each interviewer for his or her business card.

## AFTER THE INTERVIEW

Civility may not be dead, but it is, arguably, on life support. In light of
this, be one of the very few—or the only candidate—who takes time and
thought and initiative and energy to convey genuine thanks, in writing, to
the interviewer(s) for the time and interest invested in considering your
candidacy. At the same time, in the same note, state your unflagging interest and enthusiasm. The actual power of genuine civility and kindness is
underrated by so many candidates that your thoughtful message of thanks
can help you stand out from most or even all of your competition. This
usually ignored action has decided many close calls among closely matched
finalists.

If during the interview you asked the important question, "Where are
you now in your process?", then you are well positioned to use the response to more ably determine whether to send your written message of
thanks by snail mail or fax or e-mail, or text or tweet or LinkedIn, or
hand delivery, or some thoughtful combination of these methods, to maximize the prospect your message is read by the recipient(s) in advance of
final selection.

Many candidates express frustration and curiosity about repeatedly getting the interview and yet not getting the job. Here is a powerful, little-known strategy you can adopt and use to endeavor to learn what is going on. In the event all indications suggest an employer has selected another candidate for the position of interest, call the hiring manager, ideally at a time of day when you're most likely to reach the person directly, and:

1. Genuinely wish the employer well with the selected candidate.
2. In your own style, ask: "Completely off the record, and so I can learn from this experience, what can I do more effectively going forward?"
3. Stop talking, and listen carefully to the response.
4. Resist the urge, if any, to get defensive or critique the response.
5. Simply extend genuine thanks for the feedback and time.

Such inquiries are quite often met with generosity and candor. Most important, the information collected generally helps candidates figure out if there are persistent issues they need to know about, so straightforward corrective action can be taken. Sometimes, a candidate discovers no corrective measures are required: Another candidate's training, skills, and experience simply met the requirements more closely (e.g., the person hired has more years of experience or more advanced training). If action is needed to enhance your competitiveness, take care to not confuse this finding with a moral failing or character defect or fatal flaw; instead, take the course, get the experience, and/or brush up on this or that, as needed, to improve your game.

# You're the Carpenter

This and other books, websites, videos, software, assessment instruments, even counselors and coaches are merely tools in a toolbox. You are the carpenter. The choices are yours. The process of examining and developing your skills, interests, and values, and actively constructing a career in light of these is a process owned 100 percent by you. I encourage you to wear this book out and let the building begin.

# APPENDICES

# More Examples of Effective Position Descriptions/Blurbs

View the following examples as food for thought, not material to be copied into your résumé. Notice the unique accomplishments of each candidate. Because of this uniqueness, there exists no single blurb for every paralegal or every project manager or every coordinator or every nurse or every person in any position. Anyone who tells you otherwise (and gives you pages of boilerplate material to plop into your résumé) is underestimating your uniqueness. Employers can usually discern the difference between a thoughtlessly copied generic description and a genuine one resulting from careful thought. As the reader, you can infer a variety of skills from the following examples. The blurbs contain no vague claims of skills (i.e., no hollow self-puffery; see Chapter 4)—just concrete examples providing clear evidence of skills in action.

If presented on an 8½ × 11-inch résumé page with one-inch margins, most of the following examples (1) use no more than six lines of text, the most that's needed to convey the highlights of nearly any position, and (2) contain no orphans (single words appearing on the last line of a blurb). As you craft your unique blurbs, keep them within six lines of copy and avoid orphans.

7/06–present         Company A, Metropolis, NY
                     Director of Treasury Sales
Direct foreign exchange and money market product sales. Launch global
sales initiatives, using multisite synergies to increase margins by $6M.
Successfully integrate 2 culturally disparate sales forces and streamline
processes, resulting in 200% margin increase and smaller staff able to
serve 57% more customers. Lead e-commerce implementation project
team. Collaborate with legal staff to design and communicate changes
needed to conform to complex and changing accounting standards.

6/06–8/06            Hospital B, Metropolis, NY
                     Occupational Therapy Aide
Built thriving occupational therapy program for unit of 32 long-term
patients with schizophrenia. Persuaded doubtful colleagues of program
value by generating rapid, observable positive results.

10/03–6/06           Company C, Metropolis, NY
                     Vice President, Foreign Exchange Sales Manager
Re-engineered foreign exchange desk to handle added volume without
added staff. Managed trade shows and seminars. Co-led risk
management systems team to source and implement front- and back-
end systems and manage accounting and reconciliation issues.
Centralized order system to create a genuine 24-hour global network,
eliminating need for separate European night desk. Trained 100+ new
dealers.

4/12–present         Non-profit D, Metropolis, NY
                     Coordinator, Search and Placement, X Program
Help persons with physical and/or mental illnesses move themselves
from welfare to work. Institute "Active Seeker Agreement," statement of
requirements for candidates and staff. Streamline procedures to
eliminate excess paper, generate accurate data, and meet changing city,
state, and federal requirements. Establish phone/PC/resource bank. Co-
develop pre-employment curriculum. Manage pre-employment trainer,
job developers, retention staff, interns, and volunteers. Serve as Acting
Director in absence of director.

4/13–present        Company E, Metropolis, NY
                    Vice President, Operations
Apply planning to inventory control, import/export operations, and HR.
Integrate systems to provide instant tariff updates, transaction reports,
and cost analyses. Reduce headcount by 30% in 24 months. Manage
relationships with manufacturing, fulfillment, and distribution vendors.
Implement protocols to meet food/drug, agriculture, and customs
requirements in 30 countries. Obtain highest U.S. Customs compliance
ratings. Direct website design to give clients real-time delivery and
account data.

2/08–8/14           Hospital F, Metropolis, NY
                    Occupational Therapist, XYZ Psychiatric Clinic
Provided treatment to all acute/homicidal/suicidal inpatients of mixed
age and diagnoses. Taught theories and roles of psychiatric occupational
therapy to rotating medical staff. Supervised 15 students. Facilitated Life
Skills groups for long-term chronic populations emphasizing stress
management, time management, social skills, motivation, leisure
planning, and problem solving. Coordinated multidisciplinary treatment.

10/00–present       Non-profit Agency G, Metropolis, NY
                    Director, XYZ Program
Turn around failing program to help persons with physical and/or
mental illnesses move themselves from welfare to work. Examine
operations, establish clear requirements, and train/replace staff as
needed to (1) prevent program closure and (2) efficiently perform
assessment, medical review, case management, education (ABE/GED/
ESL/PC Skills/Pre-employment), search and placement, retention, and
billing. Generate accurate data to meet changing city, state, and federal
requirements. Manage/develop 40 staff.

9/11–6/14           Mortgage Company H, Paris, France
                    Manager of European Transactions
Audited debtor firms to facilitate prevention of defaults and
bankruptcies. Examined operations of Swiss bank targeted for purchase.
Connected French entrepreneurs with suitable lenders.

8/09–9/11          Company I, Paris, France
                   Executive Vice President and Managing Director
Managed the import, marketing, sale, and distribution of decorative
articles. Directed US$8M in sales, 4 offices, and 20 employees.

9/08–present       Medical Company J, Metropolis, NY
                   Senior Information Consultant
Provide all research. Establish Information Center procedures to serve 6
sites. Maintain electronic filing system. Prepare and implement
recommendations on projects ranging from systems migrations to
storage requirements.

1/08–11/09         Food Company K, Metropolis, NY
                   Data Consultant, Business Information Services
Participated in development of intranet catalog. Refined, updated, and
expanded classification scheme and corporate taxonomies. Designed
customized tools to create hierarchies and monitor accuracy and
consistency.

10/03–1/08         Medical Company L, Metropolis, NY
                   Information Consultant, Decision Support Services
Rapidly fulfilled complex information requests using print and
electronic resources. Gained expertise in organizational and knowledge
management activities.

6/04–8/05          Holding Company M, Metropolis, NY
                   Legal Assistant, Assistant to Corporate Secretary
Processed Securities and Exchange Commission filings. Summarized
depositions. Performed case cite checking. Maintained litigation files.
Recorded and tracked employee stock purchases.

8/10–present      Technology Company N, Metropolis, NY
                  Client Relationship Manager
Define and implement procedures to serve publishers, online resellers, and end-users of applications software for Xs [electronic devices]. Manage client service staff. Select and implement use of salesforce.com to log calls. Source, extensively train, and remotely supervise India call center vendor to meet 1 major client's requirements.

8/12–6/14         Bank O, Metropolis, NY
                  Operations Specialist
Converted from temporary to permanent based on performance. Processed mortgage applications. Performed credit checks. Created database to track existing loan files.

2/99–8/09         Moving Company P, Rome, Italy and Paris, France
                  President
Provided moving services to French military. Managed $10M in sales, 3 offices, and 35 staff.

12/06–present     Company Q, Metropolis, NY and Paris, France
11/08–present     General Director, Metropolis, NY
Create first U.S. store for French retail fashion chain. Manage all real estate, merchandising, staffing, marketing, and accounting. Achieve sales of $500/square foot. Serve as liaison with Paris headquarters.
12/06–11/08       NY General Director, Paris, France
Obtained orientation and training in all business areas at corporate headquarters.

6/97–5/98         Bank R, Metropolis, NY
                  Vice President, Chief Forward Dealer
Designed and implemented first online, real-time system to provide position, profitability, and gap analyses for all foreign exchange exposures. Strengthened communication between traders and IT staff to test new applications. Managed strategic and foreign exchange trading desks.

5/09–7/10          Bank S of England, Metropolis, NY
                   Senior Foreign Exchange Dealer
Managed cross-currency and strategic trading desks. Designed foreign
exchange training program. Trained 21 new dealers.

6/07–5/10          Retail Chain T, Metropolis, NY
                   Assistant Store Manager
Trained and managed 150. Supervised merchandising, customer service,
personnel, cash control, and internal and external loss prevention.
Monitored local competition and adjusted pricing and presentation as
needed. Audited 2 sites to ensure compliance with laws, company
standards, policies, and procedures.

3/03–12/05         Health Food Store U, Metropolis, NY
                   Community Outreach Coordinator
Created and delivered seminars and workshops on health and nutrition
awareness to educators, students, homemakers, and community
organizations. Collaborated with area non-profits (e.g., American Heart
Association, YMCA) and hospitals (e.g., XYZ Hospital) in support of
their respective missions.

2/11–5/13          Company V, Hong Kong
                   Consultant
Conducted in-depth economic research to assess viability of client
investments. Helped clients negotiate complex licensing and partnership
agreements and plan investment projects.

| 7/93–4/99 | Cable Company W, |
|---|---|
| | Hong Kong and Johannesburg, South Africa |
| 2/98–4/99 | General Manager, Sales and Marketing, |
| | Johannesburg, South Africa |

Directed all business development, including planning and marketing strategies. Managed introduction, pricing, promotion, and branding of telecomm services. Defined, recommended, and managed upgrade of customer service and billing system, in advance of deadline and under budget. Favorably renegotiated terms with local venture partners, forming Cable XYZ (South Africa) Ltd. Reported directly to CEO.

| 2/95–2/98 | Deputy Chief Representative, |
|---|---|
| | Johannesburg, South Africa |

Served as second-in-command of all business development. Built solid political support, successfully petitioning government for permission to rapidly establish offices. Developed alliances, partners, and new business, helping establish firm nationally as recognized industry leader. Negotiated US$207M venture project with dominant state-owned carrier. Prospected and closed competitive US$1M gateway access deal for client. Met stringent regulations of local and national government agencies.

| 7/93–1/95 | Assistant Manager, Business Development, |
|---|---|
| | Hong Kong |

Formulated and implemented strategies to expand business to South Africa. Identified, built, and expanded relationships with local partners and corporate clients. Conducted successful presentations and training programs, persuading local partners and national government of benefits of foreign investment. Researched and evaluated investment opportunities. Created business proposals with demand and revenue forecasts. In 1 year, doubled client base for international voice and data services.

4/89–8/93          X University, Metropolis, NY
                   Administrator, Graduate Recruitment
Introduced software to improve applicant-screening process. Trained
colleagues on use of office applications. Managed complex logistics for
high volume of candidates and screeners. Organized results of PC-based
Myers-Briggs personal style measure. Designed recruitment literature
and managed its production and distribution. Performed outreach to
universities and recruiters.

4/86–4/89          Company Y, Metropolis, NY
                   Administrator, Business Information Unit
Automated interlibrary loan system. Searched, retrieved, and maintained
research for worldwide staff. Extracted relevant data from daily
newspapers to create timely organizational bulletins.

8/95–8/96          Retail Chain Z, Metropolis, NY
                   Front-End Manager
Managed cashiers, cash office, bridal registry, monogramming, and gift
wrapping services.

8/02–present        Non-profit A, Metropolis, NY
                    Instructor, ABE (Adult Basic Education) and
                    GED (General Educational Development)
Provide ABE and GED instruction to help persons with physical and/or
mental illnesses move themselves from welfare to work. Strive to (1) set
example by attendance, promptness, boundaries, and social skills and
(2) create a safe space, an environment of mutual respect, and kindness
conducive to active learning.

10/99–7/02         Non-profit B, Metropolis, NY
                   Instructor, Job Readiness
Initiated and facilitated work-based education including job readiness,
life skills, ABE, and ESL (English as a Second Language) for difficult-to-
employ adults. Developed intra-agency work experience sites for
students. Trained, evaluated, and mentored interns with barriers to
competitive employment.

9/97–7/99          Non-profit C, Metropolis, NY
                   Pre-employment Trainer, Supervisor of
                   Employment Specialists
Managed 4 staff in service of moving persons with developmental
challenges into supported work settings. Initiated and crafted
curriculum for and facilitated pre-employment training. Edited pitches
to employers, including testimonials and tax credit data. Met city, state,
and federal reporting requirements.

5/97–10/00         Non-profit D, Metropolis, NY
                   Consultant (part-time)
Analyzed 50 businesses owned/operated by consumers with mental
illnesses. Implemented changes to cut costs and raise revenues.
Established protocols for budgets and contract and grant administration.
Wrote ~$300K in successful grant proposals. Served as Acting Director
of XYZ Housing (5/97–4/98), a 50-unit scattered site apartment program. Designed and supervised vocational program for psychiatric and
substance-abusing tenants. Conducted home visits including functional
assessments, behavioral contracting, and cognitive and vocational
screenings. Managed 4 case managers and 2 staff.

8/93–5/96          Petroleum Company E, London, England
                   Administrator, Organization Effectiveness Unit
Appraised security and reception functions. Organized travel, meetings,
and worldwide conferences for 40 executives. Assembled, produced,
and monitored budget. Prepared and delivered presentations.
Supervised 6 staff.

8/95–12/96         Law Firm F, Metropolis, NY
                   Legal Assistant
Prepared certificates of incorporation, merger and acquisition
documents.

5/86–present       Financial Services Company G, Metropolis, NY
7/98–present       Vice President, Administration & Financial Reporting
Develop and support custom applications for Controllers to meet
complex weekly, monthly, year-end, and ad hoc management reporting
requirements. Provide clear, easy-to-use menu-driven interfaces.
Standardize reporting to increase process efficiencies.
12/94–7/98         Assistant Vice President, Strategic Business &
                   Evaluation Group
Designed quarterly client revenue and product revenue tracking
systems. Collected data from internal and external sources to create
integrated decision-making tools for senior executives. Created
headcount reporting and analysis tool for Human Resources. Produced
intranet content for CFO with detailed corporate budget guidelines.
2/92–12/94         Associate, Distributed Financial Systems
Managed migration of budget system from mainframe to client/server
environment. Served as liaison among programmers and financial
analyst to develop reporting and maintenance utilities.
6/89–2/92          Technical Support
Thrived amid departmental transitions (serving both Distributed
Application/Technology Support and Corporate Budgeting), in service of
forecasts/budgets in client/server environment.
5/86–6/89          Systems Analyst, Corporate Budget
Trained and supported all levels of management on computing. Created
graphically advanced financial presentations. Participated in migration
to Windows operating system in LAN environment. Evaluated and
recommended suitable software applications and hardware.

6/96–present      Manufacturing Company H, Metropolis, NY
10/99–present     Manager of Information Services and Webmaster
Lead team to provide Web-based solutions for multiple constituencies
and initiatives. Manage e-business strategic plans for intranet sites.
Collaborate on content management, portals, and document
management. Chair 80-member group on data management and
business intelligence.
3/97–10/99        Information Specialist and Webmaster
Wrote *XYZ* for 500+ staff. Served as Editor of *Compliance Quarterly*.
Managed secretary, interns, and vendors. Produced content for,
maintained, and marketed 3 websites. Provided custom research for
senior staff in response to 1,200+ requests/year.
6/96–3/97      Librarian
Initiated and developed Quality & Compliance Services Library in
service of worldwide quality and regulatory affairs staff. Managed
cataloging, acquisition/collection development and budget.

2/98–11/99        X Device Services Company I, London, England
                  General Manager and Manager, Technical Support
Managed 8. Introduced and enforced protocols for technical support,
human resources, finance, and advertising. Selected and adapted new
accounting application (Sage) to facilitate coherent reporting on all
aspects of transactions. Installed software (Office Talk) to more
efficiently manage e-mails and client service schedules. Designed and
maintained website. Designed ads and vigorously promoted firm's
services. Trained staff and clients in use of X brand devices.

12/96–4/99        Title Company J, Metropolis, NY
                  Project Manager
Managed 400+ UCC filings/week. Prepared files to meet complex
jurisdictional requirements. Coordinated searches. Met time-sensitive
requirements of attorneys and paralegals. Trained 8.

8/99–present        Computer Service Company K, Metropolis, NY
                    Owner and Computer Technician
Install, configure, upgrade, diagnose, troubleshoot, repair, and perform
preventive maintenance on PCs and associated operating systems,
applications software, printers, peripherals, and networks. Serve as local
subcontractor for manufacturer warranty work. Meet and exceed
numerous service standards. Maintain financial records. Create ads and
earn referrals to obtain direct clients.

9/92–present        Self-employed, Metropolis, NY
                    Guest Lecturer, Subject X (part-time)
Teach at New York University (NYU), Mercy College, Dominican
College, Long Island University (LIU), and State University of New York
(SUNY) Health Science Center at Brooklyn (aka Downstate Medical
Center).

9/81–6/85           Metropolis University, Metropolis, NY
                    Teaching Assistant, Biophysics (part-time)
Conducted advanced biophysics seminars for physicians/full professors/
doctoral candidates.

1/96–5/98           Metropolis Cable Network, Metropolis, NY
                    Account Executive
Generated $3M in new business. Tripled revenues from $500K to
$1.5M. Clients included BMW, UPS, Benetton, Kodak, and Sprint.

2/94–12/95          *Metropolis Magazine*, Metropolis, NY
                    Sales Representative
Developed and built up Home Furnishings, Entertainment, and Atlantic
City categories. Sold over 100 pages of advertising/year.

[In the next example, notice the choice to emphasize customer service instead of merchandising.]

| | |
|---|---|
| 8/93–9/94 | Retail Chain L, Metropolis, NY |
| 10/93–9/94 | Assistant Merchandise Manager |
| 8/93–10/93 | Customer Service Supervisor |

Supervised schedules, front-end, store safe, petty cash, deposits, and seasonal department. Managed up to 50 staff. Shared Operations Manager duties, including recruiting, training, supplies, and maintenance.

[Notice in this next example that not every position requires a blurb.]

| | |
|---|---|
| 1/95–10/99 | United States Army, Hospital M, Fort ABC, NY |
| 3/98–10/99 | Head Nurse, Family Practice Clinic |

Managed high-volume operation with 400+ clients/week. Served as liaison among patients, families, providers, and vendors.

| | |
|---|---|
| 2/96–2/98 | Labor and Delivery Staff Nurse |

Supervised 4. Conducted childbirth education classes. Participated in new product studies.

| | |
|---|---|
| 1/95–1/96 | Staff Nurse, Male Surgical Ward |

[Several positions can be summarized, as shown here, in one slightly longer-than-usual blurb.]

4/85–11/98          Company N, Metropolis, NY

After providing engineering support, sales support, and direct client care, managed 42 sales staff and established relationships with 75 external distribution firms. Routinely exceeded sales quotas. Promoted synergies among sales and operations. Established protocols to dramatically cut travel expenses. Developed and conducted sales and technical training. Selected sites and managed complex logistics for trade shows worldwide. Collaborated to create marketing literature and programs. Initiated and executed strategic plans in concert with subsidiaries.

| | |
|---|---|
| 4/93–11/98 | Director of Sales, Technical Sales, and Sales Training Programs |
| 3/91–4/93 | Manager, International Sales |
| 7/89–3/91 | Sales Specialist, International |
| 10/86–7/89 | OEM Product Sales Support Specialist |
| 4/85–10/86 | Engineering Technician |

[Here is another example describing multiple positions with one blurb. The blurb also effectively positions the candidate's exit.]

| | |
|---|---|
| 4/97–present | Company O, Metropolis, NY |
| 4/08–present | Lead Advisor, W, X, Y, and Z |

Initiate and develop applications to accelerate communication among human resources, payroll, and sales. Co-develop system to streamline sales territory assignments and changes. Develop applications for system security, contact management, account management, and direct marketing data. Evaluate and select software tools. Provide technical support to user support staff. Train users, programmers, and analysts of various skill levels. Thrive amid 4 mergers/acquisitions. Decline recent offer to join company's relocation to Iowa. Provide seamless transition to successor (TBD, estimated 1/15).

| | |
|---|---|
| 4/01–4/08 | Senior Advisor, X, Y, and Z |
| 4/99–4/01 | Systems Analyst, X and Y |
| 4/97–4/99 | Senior Programmer, X |

[Here is another example using one blurb to describe multiple positions.]

2/90–present     Company P, Tokyo, Japan

Establish Singapore presence. Recruit 600+ engineers and supervisors from 25+ countries for worldwide assignments. Manage evaluations, re-assignments, in-house sales incentives, and payroll. Negotiate leases. Meet local tax and regulatory requirements. Implement software and protocols to operate on time and under budget, earning Corporate Presidential Award for achievements. Re-deployed to evaluate, correct, and prevent critical materials delays; launch Slovakia operations; and run procurement for Iran facility. Promoted to run entire division.

| | |
|---|---|
| 9/98–present | Manager, Construction Division, Tokyo, Japan |
| 10/97–9/98 | Iran Refinery Procurement Coordinator, Tokyo, Japan |
| 6/97–9/97 | Administration Manager, Bratislava, Slovakia |
| 4/96–6/97 | Buyer, Tokyo, Japan |
| 11/95–4/96 | Special Expeditor, Tokyo, Japan |
| 4/95–11/95 | Singapore Administration Manager, Tokyo, Japan |
| 2/90–4/95 | General Manager, Singapore |

[Here is a final example using one blurb to describe multiple positions.]

7/77–8/89          Company Q, Tokyo, Japan
Wrote and edited engineering standards for company-wide use. Applied
standards knowledge to increasing role in materials management, including inventory, document control, logistics, and procurement for
4 locations. Directed US$70M budget. Sourced and negotiated complex
multinational subcontracts. Collaborated on elaborate presentations to
update clients and facilitate new projects. Implemented new software to
streamline operations, earning Award for Excellence in Technology Application.
4/88–8/89          Manager, Marketing Materials, Tokyo, Japan
4/87–4/88          Controls Manager, Safwa, Saudi Arabia
5/85–4/87          Assistant Controls Manager, Tokyo, Japan and
                   Safwa, Saudi Arabia
5/83–5/85          Administration Supervisor, Tokyo, Japan
1/83–5/83          Project Control Staff, Tokyo, Japan
11/79–1/83         Assistant Controls Manager, Tokyo, Japan and
                   Safwa, Saudi Arabia
7/77–11/79         Writer and Editor, Standards and Manuals,
                   Tokyo, Japan

[Notice how lateral and downward position changes (in lieu of layoff) are
handled in this next example.]

1/79–3/89          Company R, Metropolis, NY
Co-developed and implemented contracts administration staff training
adopted for nationwide use. Conveyed training in print, by phone, and
in person. Cut service response times by evaluating problems and
swiftly deploying suitably skilled technicians to clients. Thrived amid
complex organizational changes. Served in 7 positions, ranging from
Receptionist to Regional Contracts Administrator.

[Notice how an "additive promotion" with dual responsibilities is explained here.]

| 12/79–3/93 | Company S, Metropolis, NY |
| 1/88–3/93 | Director of Operations |

While continuing to serve as Traffic Manager, also managed complex trades, hedging physical position against futures position to profitably negotiate coffee imports and sales to domestic manufacturers. Initiated creation of relational database to track transactions, including inventory, delivery, and invoicing.

| 12/79–1/88 | Traffic Manager |

Directed coffee imports and national distribution network. Negotiated freight contracts with more than 30 trucking, rail, and ocean carriers. Managed relationships with 13 external warehouses across the country. Obtained approvals from U.S. Customs, U.S. FDA, and clientele with rigorous product standards.

[Notice, next, how the "additive promotion" from supervisor to assistant director is handled.]

8/94–10/00          Hospital T, Metropolis, NY
10/98–10/00         Clinical Director,
                    Occupational/Recreational/Arts Therapies
Planned and directed clinical services and managed budgets for 15 psychiatric and substance abuse programs. Initiated agreements with 25 schools to engage 100+ graduate/undergraduate occupational therapy students. Managed Continuous Quality Improvement for Psychiatry Department. Managed 23.
10/96–10/98         Assistant Director,
                    Occupational/Recreational/Arts Therapies
Supervisor role extended to second facility (Hospital X).
8/94–9/96           Supervisor,
                    Occupational/Recreational/Arts Therapies
Reorganized for more cost-effective and integrated services in drug/alcohol/women's detoxification inpatient and dual diagnosis outpatient programs. Initiated quality assurance measures. Supervised 8 therapists. Trained staff on managed care protocols. Managed caseload. Conducted in-service training. Authored—and trained staff to use—*ABCDE Workbook* for persons with mental illness and chemical addiction. Designed, conducted, presented, and published research. Served as Acting Director in absence of program director.

# A Special Note to Homemakers

Regardless of gender, if you are returning to paid work or seeking paid work for the first time, you may think you don't have the skills needed to thrive in today's competitive job market.

Hmm . . . let's look at the facts. Homemakers have many skills to offer. Smart employers look beyond paid work to any evidence of transferable skills. Here is a sample position description/blurb (much larger than is appropriate for an actual résumé) containing many examples of action statements for homemakers. Each action statement gives the reader specific evidence of transferable skills. Use these examples as food for thought as you craft your own action statements unique to you.

On an 8½ × 11-inch résumé page with one-inch margins, keep your position description/blurb to within six lines and avoid orphans (single words appearing on the last line of a blurb).

> 1/00–present      Homemaker, Metropolis, NY
> Manage schedules and logistics for family of 5. Balance priorities to create and implement budget. Motivate, coach, and counsel children. Teach and model ethics. Work with teachers to closely monitor academic performance of children. Plan, organize, and co-supervise extracurricular school activities. Mediate disputes among family members and facilitate solutions. Shop for clothing, food, and supplies.

(continues)

> Prepare and serve nutritious meals for 5. Coordinate medical care for all family members. Establish clear requirements and discipline children. Drive children to schools, team sports, music lessons, and more. Negotiate with suppliers. Pay invoices. Reconcile accounts. Arrange for home and vehicle maintenance and repairs. Maintain clean home and clean clothes for family. Plan and create dinners to entertain mate's employers, colleagues, clients, and prospects. Collaborate with mate to manage investments.

Clearly, it takes a variety of skills to make a home and nurture others. It is obvious to any reader that many of these skills are transferable to paid work. Thus, there is no reason to omit or otherwise disguise or downplay the role of homemaker on your résumé. Rather than hide it, tell it—tell employers this important element of your unique story.

# A Special Note to Veterans

Write for readers who have little or no understanding of the military. Use plain English, civilian terminology.

As you write, omit/exclude:

- Military terminology/jargon
- Military acronyms
- Military slang
- Military abbreviations
- Details of combat

Since you are transitioning into a new career, include a Goal section (see Chapter 4).

Create position descriptions/blurbs containing plenty of action statements (i.e., evidence of transferable skills)* and get specific. For example, describe:

---

*Go to *www.google.com*, *www.zoo.com*, or *www.duckduckgo.com* and search for "military to civilian skills" until you find among the search results free translation sites providing military position descriptions and the civilian versions of those descriptions. Do not cut and paste the material from such sites into your résumé. Instead, use the information as food for thought as you devise civilian-friendly action statements for your unique document.

- Number of people managed
- Dollar amounts of budgets managed
- Dollar value of assets you managed
- "Civilian-transferable" skills training you have *given* to others
- Problems/opportunities successfully identified and acted upon
- Security clearances given to you (e.g., high-risk public trust, confidential, secret, or top secret)

In an Education section, include training you have *received*, but be selective. For example, omit training in marksmanship (unless you seek law enforcement work) and hand-to-hand combat, but include courses in logistics, technology, or the many other areas readily transferable to civilian work.

Find and carefully review any written evaluations you have received; these documents often contain useful food for thought when writing a résumé.

When getting your résumé reviewed, be sure to get civilian reviewers. Use only reviewers who 1) routinely hire people as part of their work and 2) possess writing skills and candor you respect. Ex-military people who have successfully transitioned to civilian career paths can make excellent reviewers, too.

Many free career resources for veterans are available online. For example, use your favorite search engine (e.g., *www.google.com*, *www.zoo.com*, or *www.duckduckgo.com*) to find current links to "United States Department of Veterans Affairs" and "United States Department of Labor Veterans' Preference Advisor" and "United States Department of Labor Veterans' Employment and Training Service."

If you have less than an honorable discharge (e.g., general, undesirable, bad conduct, or dishonorable), there is a chance you can have your discharge upgraded by the Discharge Review Board or the Board of Correction of Military Records of the appropriate branch of service. Contact your local legal service agency (e.g., Legal Aid Society) or Red Cross, Veterans Center, or State Division of Veterans' Affairs for help. Doing so can improve your chances with employers who request your discharge papers.

Before applying for a discharge upgrade, be sure to request, obtain, and carefully save copies of your military records from Military Personnel Records Center, 9700 Page Avenue, St. Louis, MO 63132-1547. This is important because after you apply for a discharge upgrade, your records are sealed forever; neither you nor your attorney may view them.

Old discharge papers (form DD-214) include "SPN" or "spin" numbers that can identify people with drug or alcohol problems. Many employers can translate the spin numbers, so if these are issues for you, also request from St. Louis copies of the DD-214 with the spin number deleted.

Thank you and your loved ones for your service.

# A Special Note to Ex-Offenders

Ex-offenders searching for work face plenty of challenges. What is the biggest one?

- Being banned from receiving food stamps or other financial assistance? No.
- Being banned from taking some jobs (e.g., security, medicine, childcare, education)? No.
- Being unfairly discriminated against by many narrow-minded employers? No.
- Recovering from substance abuse?* No.
- Finding stable housing? No.
- Getting access to transportation? No.
- Getting access to healthcare? No.
- Improving basic skills?** No.
- Finding interview/work clothes?† No.

*See Appendix E: A Special Note to People in Recovery.

**Free courses are available. Go to any public library and ask for information about Adult Basic Education (ABE), General Educational Development (GED), or English for Speakers of Other Languages (ESOL).

†Free interview/work clothes are available. Go to any public library and ask for information about Bottomless Closet, Career Closet, Career Gear, Dress for Success, Working Wardrobes, and other like-minded organizations.

- Re-unification with loved ones? No.
- The belief that no employer will hire you because you are an ex-offender? Yes.

Believing that no employer will hire you because you are an ex-offender is your single biggest barrier to finding legal paid work. If you believe no employer will hire you because you are an ex-offender, you might as well stop reading; none of the following information will be of any use to you until you choose to change this belief.

Choosing to change ineffective beliefs is important. Drama inside your head can make it hard to believe in yourself and take action toward your goals. If you often have negative thoughts, argue, feel stressed, sad, or angry, there are ways to make it better. Ask your probation/parole officer to refer you to a clinical social worker or other mental health professional trained in rational emotive behavior therapy or cognitive behavioral therapy to help people think in ways that help them feel and do better. How you think about the job search (or anything else, for that matter) deeply affects results.

Once you believe—or act as if you believe, until you really do believe—that an employer will hire you, it is time to create a résumé that will honestly get your phone to ring.

As mentioned in the Introduction: Don't make stuff up. There are many reasons to not make stuff up on your résumé or on a job application. If you lie and an employer finds out, you will very likely be immediately dismissed and maybe even criminally prosecuted for "willful misrepresentation." How can an employer find out? The information may slip out. Anyone who knows or recognizes you may (1) unintentionally communicate something that reveals your offense to your employer, (2) intentionally reveal, or (3) threaten to reveal. You do not need a secret and a potential crisis hanging over your head every day.

Therefore, do not write false starting dates or ending dates (see Employment Gaps section in Chapter 1) to mask the times during which you were incarcerated. Instead, write real starting and ending dates (month and year) and focus on including on your résumé all the transferable skills you have to offer. Prior to or while serving your sentence, did you get any vocational training? Did you work? Are you skilled in woodworking, carpentry, plumbing, painting, cleaning, electrical, metal work, food prep or cooking, landscaping, operating office equipment (phone, fax, copier, or computer), bookkeeping? Did you take any classes? Can you speak, read, or write a language in addition to English? Have you done volunteer work? In what ways did you participate in pre-release programs? Honestly list your accomplishments on your résumé and on job applications.

As you transition to the job market:

- Act as if you believe—until you really do believe—an employer will hire you.
- Create—alone or with help—an honest résumé. Do not be persuaded otherwise.
- Get a disposition slip for each offense from the court of conviction so you are ready for an employer's request.
- Rap sheets often contain damaging mistakes. Request a copy of yours from the appropriate state agency, review it, and then submit original disposition slips to correct the record.
- Ask people who can attest to how your behaviors have changed for the better to serve as references. See Chapter 7. If you're playing by the rules, then your parole officer can serve as an excellent reference.
- Think about, write, and rehearse in front of a mirror at least 100 times your three-part, 60-second explanation of (1) your errors in judgment, (2) the lessons you've learned from these errors, and (3) your total commitment to a new path.
- Ask your local librarian for information on and forms for the Work Opportunity Tax Credit, and bring the forms to interviews. Give the forms to employers and explain that in addition to getting a good worker, if they hire you they can also get money (up to $2,400 at the time of this writing) from the government.
- Contact your state division of parole or, if you still have one, ask your parole officer to help you obtain certificates of rehabilitation (e.g., relief from disabilities, good conduct) that remove some restrictions on employment.
- Ask your local librarian (or call 1-800-233-2258) for your area's contact information and forms for the Federal Bonding Program. Bring this information and the forms to interviews, too. Use your judgment. If you think it will help, give the form to employers and

explain that this program helps protect employers (at no cost to them) against loss of money or property due to employer dishonesty.

- Avoid spending time with anyone who is engaged in illegal behaviors.
- Reach out to other ex-offenders who have successfully returned to legal paid work.

# A Special Note to People in Recovery

As you know, you cannot move successfully along any career path if you are using. Before you attempt to create a résumé, seek out useful tools for recovery.

One such tool is relapse prevention training. Be your own advocate; ask around until you find it. Such training will help you understand the process that can lead to relapse, identify triggers, and learn coping skills to prevent relapse.

Another proven resource is *www.smartrecovery.org*, an excellent site that provides online peer support groups, an online message board, and information on face-to-face meetings around the world.

Here are three more excellent resources:

1. *When AA Doesn't Work for You: Rational Steps to Quitting Alcohol* by Albert Ellis and Emmett Velten (Fort Lee, NJ: Barricade Books, 1992).
2. *Rational Recovery: The New Cure for Substance Addiction* by Jack Trimpey (New York: Pocket Books, 1996).
3. *Stay Sober and Straight: How to Prevent Addiction Relapse with the Rational Self-Help Treatment Method* by Maxie Maultsby (Weirton, WV: Rational Self-Help Books, 1990).

Unexplained job exits, lengthy employment gaps, and other challenging issues caused by your substance abuse are more easily explained when you are *in* recovery. If the résumé you send includes clear evidence of skills useful to an employer, then you may be invited to explain the issues. Think about, write, and rehearse in front of a mirror at least 100 times your three-part, 60-second explanation to:

- Acknowledge your total responsibility for the consequences of your substance abuse.
- Announce the period of time you have been clean—and your willingness to be tested.
- State your determination to continue to work at it for the rest of your life to stay clean.

Many employers respect the courage it takes to say and mean such things. As a result, people in recovery who are honestly committed to staying clean are hired and thriving in the workplace every day. You can be one of them.

# Index

academic degrees, 19–20
action statements, 36–38
    for homemakers, 117–118
address, 20
Adobe Reader software, 18, 58
advertising
    for filled positions, xv
    responding to blind, 60–62
ALL CAPS, 18
analytical skills, 90
answering machine, outgoing
    message on, xx
apartment number in address, 20
appearance for job interview, 84, 87–92
approximately, ~ symbol for, 30
Arial font, 17
artwork, 51
attachments to e-mail, file formats
    for, 58
attribution error, fundamental, 86
automated templates, xviii

black ink, 13
blank lines, font point size for, 15
blind ads, responding to, 60–62

Board of Correction of Military
    Records, 120
boldface, 17
borders on résumé, 51
branchout.com, 12
brevity, xvii–xviii, 6
bullets, 28–29
business cards, 92
buzzwords, xviii

*Career Interests Game* (University
    of Missouri), 4*n*
career path, 4, 5
careercloud.com, 12
careers, changing, 23
careersonar.com, 12
Carnegie, Dale, *How to Win Friends
    and Influence People*, 87
cell phone, 20–21, 85
characters, space between, 15–16
chronological résumé, vs. functional, 7
civilian terminology, for military
    experience, 119
civility, 92
claims, avoiding vague, 24–26

communication, effective, 6
confidence, 67
confidentiality agreements, 11
constructive criticism, 90
consumer.ftc.gov, 75
content, vs. delivery system, xiii
cooperative verbs, 30
courtesy, 87
cover letters, 65–72
    contact information on, 66
    error-free, 65–70
    length of, 66–67
    samples, 68
critiques, from résumé sellers, xix
Crosby, Philip, *Quality Is Free: The Art
    of Making Quality Certain*, 87
curriculum vitae (CV), 7

dates, 28
deadlines, 89
decorative borders, 51
delivery systems, xiii
descriptive blurb for positions, 29,
    33–34
    samples, 34–35
Discharge Review Board, 120
.doc file format, 58
.docx file format, 18
dreamkillers, 5

education on résumé, 27, 46–47
    military training listed in, 120
electronic scanners, xix
*The Elements of Style* (Strunk
    and White), xix
elevator speech, 34
Ellis, Albert
    *A Guide to Rational Living*, 82
    *How to Control Your Anger Before
    It Controls You*, 9–10
    *When AA Doesn't Work for You*,
    127

e-mail
    file formats for attachments,
    58
    including résumé in body, 59
    signature, 21–22
e-mail address, 14, 21
    determining company from, 61
employers
    decision maker preferences, xvi
    interest from targeted, next steps, 83
    location for, 28
    preferences, 57$n$
    temporary agencies as, 29–30
    using resources of, 20–21, 88
employment application
    lies on, 124
    online, 59–60
    public-sector, 8$n$
employment gaps, 7–8
enthusiasm, 67, 89
    of possible reference, 78
entrepreneurs, 9
envelopes, printing, 48
exaggeration of facts, xviii
executive summary, 24
ex-offenders, 123–126
experts, informational interview
    requests of, 70–72

facial feedback hypothesis, 85
Fair Credit Reporting Act, 75
fax number, 21, 61
Federal Bonding Program, 125
file formats, 18
    for e-mail attachments, 58
fonts, 16–17
    point size for blank lines, 15
functional résumé, vs. chronological, 7
fundamental attribution error, 86

GED (General Educational
    Development), 47

goals, 23
    ability to speak about, 90
    of interpersonal effectiveness, 86
    vs. objective, 24
grade point average (GPA), 46
*A Guide to Rational Living* (Ellis), 82

halo effect, 86
header for résumé, 6
headhunters, xvi, 61
headings, spacing content under, 16
hiring, describing reason for, 91
hiring manager
    call for name, 66
    feedback from, 93
hiring process, learning stage of,
    92
homemakers, 117–118
honesty, 89, 124
*How to Control Your Anger Before
    It Controls You* (Ellis and
    Tafrate), 9–10
*How to Win Friends and Influence
    People* (Carnegie), 87
humor, in cover letters, risk of, 67

informational interview request
    letter, 70–72
ink, 13–14
inquiry letter, 3, 59, 69–70
    sample, 70
    targeted, 3
interim jobs, 8
Internet access, public libraries for, 2n
Internet search engines
    to check e-mail address, 21
    to check phone number, 20
interpersonal skills, improving, 87
interview, reasons resume does
    not result in, xv–xvi
inventions, 47–48
italics, 18

jargon, xviii
jewelry, 84
job application
    lies on, 124
    online, 59–60
    public-sector, 8n
job hopping, 9–10
job interview, 84
    appearance for, 84, 87–92
    displaying desired qualities, 88–91
    follow-up, 92–93
    mental preparation, 85–86
    physical preparation, 84–85
job/career fairs, 60
jobon.com, 60

Kagan, Elena, xiv
kerning, 15–16
Kindle smart phone software, 18

language skills, 49
lateral position changes, description
    examples, 114
learnup.com, 83
letters
    informational interview request,
        70–72
    *see also* cover letters; inquiry letter
libraries, for Internet access, 2n
lies, on job application, 124
line art on résumé, 51
Linehan, Marsha, 86
listening, 89
locations, for sending résumés, 1
Lucht, John, *Rites of Passage at $100,000
    to $1 Million+*, 87

mailing address, 20
margins, 14
mashable.com, 12
mass mailings, avoiding, 1
Maultsby, Maxie, *Stay Sober and
    Straight*, 127

memberships, on résumé, 49–50
message, on answering machine or
    voice mail, xx
military records, saving copies of,
    120–121
monetary value, 30
MOOC (Massive Open Online
    Courses), 47n

name, for résumé file, 58
newspaper private box number, for
    blind ad, 61
numerals, vs. words, 30

objective, vs. goal, 24
online application, 59–60
operating principles of organization, 3

pager numbers, 20
paper, 13
parole, certificates of rehabilitation, 125
.pdf file format, 18, 58
per, / symbol for, 31
percent, % symbol for, 30
personal information, 50
personal name, 19
phone number, 20–21
photos, 51
phrases to avoid, 31–33
piercings, 84
position descriptions, 28–36
    examples, 99–116
    examples for lateral and downward
        changes, 114
    examples for multiple positions,
        112–114
post office box
    avoiding use of, 20
    for blind ad, 61
postage meter, 58n
presentation, 13–18
printing envelopes, 48
prison, finding work after, 123–126
privacy settings, in social media, 11

professional experience, vs. work
    experience, 27
project management, 91
proofreading, xix, 65
prospective employers, free sites for
    locating, 2
public libraries, for Internet access, 2n
public-sector employment application,
    8n
published works, 47–48

Quality Is Free: The Art of Making
    Quality Certain (Crosby), 87

Rational Recovery: The New Cure for
    Substance Addiction (Trimpey),
    127
recovery, people in, 127–128
recruiters, on employment gaps, 8
reference, asking someone to be, 77
references statement, 50, 77–79
rehabilitation, certificates of, 125
relapse prevention training, 127–128
remote interviews, 87–88
requirements for career, 4
respect, 87
résumés
    avoiding multiple, xviii
    length of, 5
    review by others, 66
    samples, 52–55
reverse job/career fairs, 60
risks, in social media, 11
Rites of Passage at $100,000 to $1
    Million+ (Lucht), 87

salary history
    compensation elements, 75, 77
    request for, 74–75
    sample, 76
salary requirements, 61–62
    request for, 73–74
sans-serif fonts, 16–17
self-employment, 9

self-respect, 86
seminars, 47–48
sending résumé, 57–60
    alternative formats and delivery
        methods, 62–63
    by multiple methods, 58
sentences, 36–38
    verb/action word for beginning,
        23, 30, 38–45
serif fonts, 16
signature, in cover letter, 67
size
    of fonts, 17
    of organization, 3
skills
    providing evidence of useful, 26–27
    transferable, 117
Skype, 21, 88
smartrecovery.org, 127
smiling, 85
snail mail, avoiding as first method, 58
social media, xiii, 10–12
software skills, résumé list of, 48–49
spacing, 14–16
    creating on first page, 15
spell-check, 65
    limitations, xix
"spin" numbers, on military discharge
        papers, 121
stapled pages, 6
*Stay Sober and Straight* (Maultsby), 127
Strunk, William, *The Elements of Style*,
        xix
substance abuse, those in recovery,
        127–128

tabs, formatting with, 14–15
Tafrate, Raymond Chip, *How to
        Control Your Anger Before It
        Controls You*, 9–10
targets, for résumés, 1–3
tattoos, 84
team work, 91
techcrunch.com, 12

technological change, 91
templates, automated, xviii
temporary agency, as employer,
        29–30
text file format, 18, 59
thank-you note for interviewer, 92
theworknumber.com, 75
time, consumption by social media, 12
Times New Roman font, 17
titles of positions, 28
transferable skills, 117
Trimpey, Jack, *Rational Recovery:
        The New Cure for Substance
        Addiction*, 127
.txt file format, 18, 59
typingtest.com, 48

underline, 18
    for e-mail address, 14
Univers font, 17
University of Missouri, *Career Interests
        Game*, 4n
*U.S. Occupational Outlook Handbook*,
        4n

vague claims, avoiding, 24–26
vehicle, appearance for interview, 84
Velton, Emmett, *When AA Doesn't
        Work for You*, 127
verb/action word, for beginning
        sentences, 23, 30, 38–45
veterans, 119–121
    career resources for, 120
voice mail, outgoing message on, xx
volunteer experience, 46

weakness, describing, 91–92
websites
    consumer.ftc.gov, 75
    jobon.com, 60
    learnup.com, 83
    for locating prospective employers, 2
    smartrecovery.org, 127
    on social media, 12

theworknumber.com, 75
typingtest.com, 48
*When AA Doesn't Work for You*
　　(Ellis and Velton), 127
White, E.B., *The Elements of Style*,
　　xix
Word document file format, 18, 58
words to avoid, 31–33

work, in self- definition, 81–82
work experience, 27
　　vs. professional experience, 27
Work Opportunity Tax Credit, 125
work resources, 20–21, 88
written materials, importance of, xiv

Zip code, 20

# About the Author

Scott Bennett has read more than 100,000 résumés, conducted thousands of interviews, and hired and developed hundreds of employees at all levels in organizations ranging in size from 3 to 34,000 people. In 1996, he transitioned from his role as President and Chief Operating Officer of Public Service Computer Software, Inc., into career coaching. Individually and in seminars and workshops, he has coached thousands of active career seekers from more than 100 countries. After launching the Career Services Office at Baruch College School of Public Affairs in New York City, he developed the site now known as *writeresumesright.com* to provide free information, tools, and resources for active career seekers.

Bennett earned a B.S. in Economics from Clark University, an M.S. in Education (specializing in Counseling and Personnel Services) from Fordham University, an M.S.W. from Silberman School of Social Work at Hunter College, and an Advanced Post-Masters Certificate in Rational Emotive and Cognitive Behavioral Therapy from Albert Ellis Institute.

In addition to his role as career coach, Bennett is a Board Certified Diplomate in Clinical Social Work, credentialed by the American Board of Examiners in Clinical Social Work. After completing two 12-month Post-MSW Fellowships awarded by the Department of Psychiatry at Yale University School of Medicine, he then joined the staff at Yale-New Haven Psychiatric Hospital. He plans to launch in fall 2014 an expanded practice to provide career coaching *and* group psychotherapy. He lives in New Haven, Connecticut.